ROBERT VENTURI'S
ROME

T0364247

ORO Editions
Publishers of Architecture, Art, and Design
Gordon Goff: Publisher
www.oroeditions.com
info@oroeditions.com
Published by ORO Editions
Copyright © ORO Editions, Stephen Harby, and Frederick Fisher 2018
Text and Images © Frederick Fisher and Stephen Harby 2018

Graphic Design: Pablo Mandel
Typeset in Trajan, Minion Pro, and Bau OT

Text: Frederick Fisher and Stephen Harby
Images: Stephen Harby and Frederick Fisher
Project Coordinator: Kirby Anderson

10 9 8 7 6 5 4 3 2

Library of Congress data available upon request. World Rights: Available

ISBN: 978-1-939621-87-0

Color Separations and Printing: ORO Group Ltd.
Printed in China.

International Distribution: www.oroeditions.com/distribution

ORO Editions makes a continuous effort to minimize the overall carbon footprint of its publications. As part of this goal, ORO Editions, in association with Global ReLeaf, arranges to plant trees to replace those used in the manufacturing of the paper produced for its books. Global ReLeaf is an international campaign run by American Forests, one of the world's oldest nonprofit conservation organizations. Global ReLeaf is American Forests' education and action program that helps individuals, organizations, agencies, and corporations improve the local and global environment by planting and caring for trees.

Cover Illustration: Casa Girasole, Luigi Moretti, Rome, 1950, Watercolor by Frederick Fisher

Robert Venturi's
ROME

FREDERICK FISHER AND STEPHEN HARBY

ORO
EDITIONS

Contents

Authors' Acknowledgements

I first experienced Rome in 1964, at the age of nine, the ward of my parents, who I gratefully thank for my love of travel and intense engagement with so many special places of the world. Each gave me in turn the gift of engaging with the genius loci of place rooted in its visual aspects as well as its underlying character. My love of Rome—as well as all things Italian began at this time, and continues to this day—following the contours of my life, bolstered by many along the way, to whom I am grateful for the wherewithal and the facilities to reap its rewards. I have been blessed with the finest and most supportive of mentors. It was of course, Vincent Scully at Yale, who introduced me not only to *Complexity and Contradiction,* but also to the many ways of seeing and understanding the built environment. As an undergraduate major in architecture at Yale, four dedicated teachers at the time, Jim Righter, Kent Bloomer, Alec Purves, and Buzz Yudell, all in turn took me in hand, and remain close friends today. Buzz Yudell introduced me to Charles Moore, with whom I studied in graduate school and in whose office I worked for the next seventeen years. From him I absorbed the many dimensions and opportunities of an architectural life and the knowledge that creation and the appreciation of place go hand in hand. During these years, a habit of experiencing places through drawing developed in school and then grew into a passion for painting in watercolor. I am grateful to the late Lee Buckley and to Timothy Clark for leading the way into this wonderful world of color and light.

I returned to Rome in mid-career thanks to the Marion O. And Maximilian E. Hoffman Rome Prize Fellowship in Architecture at the American Academy, and thus began my immersion in earnest in the layers of Rome as well as important life changes, just as promised. I was fortunate to meet many of those whose passions for and deep knowledge of all things Roman were for me an essential guide forward. These include those at the American Academy: Adele Chatfield-Taylor, its president; the late Pina Pasquantonio, its Associate Director; Lisa Fentress, Mellon Professor; and other Roman colleagues and friends: Richard Piccolo, Davide Vitali, Heather and Vernon Minor, Judy diMaio, Wendy Artin and the late Bruno Boschin.

One rarely has the chance to teach by the side of a beloved mentor, but in 2002, Alec Purves of Yale, asked me to join him in teaching a summer course in Rome for graduate students, which we continued to do for fourteen years, with the unstinting support of Dean Robert A.M. Stern. The drawings and words in these pages would not be what they are, were it not for the inspiration of sharing the city and seeing it through the eyes of over 300 Yale architecture students in the span of those years. Our course would not have been nearly as effective had it not been for the collaboration of Jeffrey Blanchard, whose lectures informed us and our students, and for whose close critical reading of this book we are most grateful. Whatever shortcomings there are in this work remain our own, and are not those of any of these others. Finally, in recent years I have had the good fortune to share my love and experiences of Rome with my husband, Kritsada Buajud, for whom it has also become *la Citta Éterna!* He has offered much patience and support during the creation of this book.

—Stephen Harby

My introduction to Rome came from the Roman architecture firm, Transit Design. In the late 1980s they needed a project architect for a Southern California project and through a mutual friend, Tom Sewel, I worked in their office on via Giulia. After dinner walks through the city, with Danilo Parisio and the late Evaristo Nicolao, gave me literally and figuratively an on-the-ground perspective of the city. *Complexity and Contradiction* was brought to my attention while studying art and art history at Oberlin College under the tutelage of Paul Arnold and Ellen Johnson. The book simply changed my career path into architecture.

I returned to Rome in 2008 thanks to the Franklin D. Israel Rome Prize, focused on Mid-Century Italian museum renovations. Franco Minissi's Etruscan Museum at the Villa Giulia is the only example of that group of museums that is in Rome. It is also one of the twenty Roman buildings cited by Venturi in *Complexity and Contradiction* (for other reasons). I gave myself the project of visiting all of the Roman buildings cited in *Complexity and Contradiction* and to study them through watercolor paintings. This process was meant to slow the time of observation. I also applied the tools of graphic analysis in contrast to Venturi's vivid words and sometimes less than vivid black and white photos.

During my study at UCLA, I attempted to maintain a balance between architecture as a vehicle for meaning as well as experience, and a celebration of the craft of model making and drawing. Computer-aided design has practically obliterated the highly personal "art of drawing" that flourished while I was at UCLA and the decade following. Coy Howard was my primary mentor in the art drawing and poetry of architecture. Tim Vreeland, founding Chair of the Graduate program, and former apprentice to Louis Kahn, brought a perspective of history.

I was lucky to be at the American Academy in Rome during the inspired leadership of Academy president, Adele Chatfield-Taylor, Rome Director, Carmello-Vircilo Franklin and the late Director of Operations, Pina Pasquantonio.

This book would not have come to fruition without my friend and co-author Stephen Harby. Stephen brought his outstanding skills as a painter, deep knowledge and insights of Rome and architecture to turn my informal studies and notes into a full-fledged pictorial and narrative essay. Shelley Santo managed this project for us with editing help from Ann Matranga. My partners and friends, David Ross and Joseph Coriaty, have collaborated with me, supported my explorations and maintained our practice from its early years.

We thank our publisher, Gordon Goff, who took on this loosely defined project and guided it into to an ORO book. Editor Kirby Anderson thoughtfully and patiently pulled the book together and designer Pablo Mandel gave it the clarity and simplicity that we sought.

My wife and partner in the Rome sojourn, Jennie Prebor, enriched the experience in countless ways with our sons, Henry and Eugene, and with her insight on everything from art history to Italian food.

—Frederick Fisher

Preface

RobertVenturi's Rome is a guidebook to the city of Rome seen through the eyes of Robert Venturi, re- interpreted by two subsequent Rome Prize fellows and architects, Frederick Fisher and Stephen Harby.

Robert Venturi wrote *Complexity and Contradiction in Architecture* at the age of 37 in 1962, after completing his fellowship at the American Academy in Rome. When it was published in 1966 by the Museum of Modern Art, Vincent Scully, renowned Professor of Art and Architecture at Yale University, called it "…probably the most important writing on the making of architecture since le Corbusier's *Vers une architecture (Toward an Architecture)* published in 1923."[1]

Venturi looks at architecture, landscape and art as different manifestations of common themes. When we were students the book was assigned to us and was fundamental to the development of our outlook on architecture as it was for most architects of our generation. Fisher read *Complexity and Contradiction* while studying art history at Oberlin College where Venturi later designed his first museum project, an addition to Cass Gilbert's Allen Art Museum. Harby read the book while studying art history and architecture at Yale. Venturi wrote the book following a two year Rome Prize fellowship at the American Academy in Rome, and there is no doubt that the city had a profound influence on his thinking. He used many buildings in Rome as examples to illustrate his theories. From the Pantheon, through works by his favorite artist, Michelangelo, and on to 20th century buildings by Armando Brasini and Luigi Moretti, Venturi reveals Rome as a complex and contradictory city.

We propose to take the reader on a journey through time and ideas by visiting and discussing nearly thirty Roman places that exemplify Venturi's revolutionary ideas. Interspersed with his ideas are our own, drawn from our practice and observations as architects. In that sense the book is an essay. It incorporates Venturi's vision with our view of the way we human beings live in a fragile relationship to nature, with our houses figuratively and sometimes literally built on ruins.

Robert Venturi's Rome is a slim volume of ten chapters, fewer than 100 pages, full of watercolor illustrations painted especially for this book. Venturi illustrated his book with small black and white photographs and drawings. Architects Stephen Harby and Frederick Fisher created imaginative and analytical watercolor illustrations for this book inspired by the original images and direct observations of buildings and urban spaces.

---

1   Robert Venturi, *Complexity and Contradiction in Architecture*, New York: The Museum of Modrn Art, 1966; Second Edition, 1977. P. 9. For the purposes of this text all page and illustration references will be to the larger format second edition.

Introduction to the Watercolors

The architectural forms that captured Venturi's attention were in most cases revealed through the play of light and shadow. When Venturi saw these buildings, often for his first time, they were still enshrouded in the dusky, atmospheric layering of many centuries of soot. The photographs he used (often classic views produced by the Alinari brothers) preserve them in that state. Today, many of the buildings can be seen in a more pristine condition, a result of the cleaning campaigns of recent years and reaching a peak for the jubilee of the millennium in 2000 and continuing to this day thanks to financial incentives.

The process to produce these watercolors reveals the effect of *chiaroscuro*, an Italian word meaning *clear/obscure* or *light/dark*. The forms are perceived in the condition of strong light, just as they were in the original photographs. When strong, direct light strikes a surface, shadows are cast by projecting elements like cornices or columns, and enable a full understanding of the three-dimensional form. The contrasting coloration of the material goes from the stark white of pristine travertine to darker tones on recessed surfaces, due to the accumulation of grime over time.

Watercolor is a transparent medium, and the expression of light is the result of "reserving" the white of the paper. This is quite different from the technique of oil or acrylic paint, where the pigment is opaque, and the expression of light depends on the use of light pigments. This is what makes watercolor both a highly challenging medium, as well as one well suited to express the play of light.

The technique used to produce views of *Robert Venturi's Rome* involves the use of successive layers of transparent sepia-toned washes, to communicate gradations of natural light reflected by the architectural forms. An area of light or white tonality relies on the maximum reflection of the white of the paper, and is "reserved" free of the application of any wash. Conversely, areas that are in shadow or dark in tone receive successive layers of the wash, or at times a dark wash less diluted with water.

Step-by-step images show the evolution of selected works in the series. To see this evolution, go to: http://www.stephenharby.com/Stephen_Harby/Venturis_Rome_Animations.html.

A Guide to the Guide

This guide is intended for all travelers to Rome, whether of the armchair or shoe leather variety, and whether the traveler is novitiate or veteran. It is said that it takes a lifetime to know Rome, and that its present day manifestation is a *palimpsest,* altered but still bearing traces of its original form. Many layers have piled up throughout Rome's recorded existence spanning three millennia. A visitor's familiarity grows with each successive contact, and as interests change over a lifetime, so too do the offerings of la *città eterna*, to satisfy the visitor's current obsession.

Venturi sums up this nature of selectivity in his Preface: "The examples chosen reflect my partiality for certain eras: Mannerist, Baroque, and Rococo especially. As Henry-Russell Hitchcock says, 'there always exists a real need to re-examine the work of the past. There is, presumably, almost always a generic interest in architectural history among architects; but the aspects, or periods, of history that seem at any given time to merit the closest attention certainly vary with changing sensibilities.'" [2]

Robert Venturi's Rome follows the organization of Venturi's own text, and buildings in Rome are presented in Venturi's order and theoretical context. We present the original citation of the building, place it within Venturi's immediate contextual argument, and then move on to present historical and factual details. The intention is to enrich the visitor's experience of the place, and conclude with a broader consideration of the building's architectural importance today, while looking back to speculate about what it meant to Venturi. In this way, our book is like the Roman god, Janus, who looks forward and back at the same time, and whose crest depicting two back-to-back human profiles was adopted by the American Academy in Rome.

The American Academy in Rome was the launching pad for Venturi's groundbreaking treatise, and also the setting that inspired one of us, Frederick Fisher, to reconsider Venturi's work when he was a Rome Prize Fellow in 2008. While the focus of Fisher's fellowship was Mid-Century Italian Museum renovations, revisiting *Complexity and Contradiction* on the ground in Rome was irresistible. Stephen Harby came to the Academy as a Fellow in 1999 to study the effects of light and shadow as framed by the architectural details of classical tradition. His watercolors in this volume are a continuation of the investigations he began at that time.

Of the nearly thirty buildings presented here, some qualify as major must-see attractions on any visitor's list, such as Saint Peter's, while others may not be as well known. Most are readily accessible to the public, or are exterior sites. Some are centrally located, while others are off the beaten path. A few

---

2   *Op. cit*, p. 13.

are not normally accessible to the public and may require some perseverance to gain access. In such cases we provide information on how to make a request for a visit, which of course, may be out of date by the time this book reaches the reader's hands. Just as Rome was not built in a day, it is hoped that the discoveries of this guide may render their rewards over a lifetime. The authors have spent their lives returning to Rome, and each visit is rewarded by some discovery or visit to a place new to them, often difficult of access.

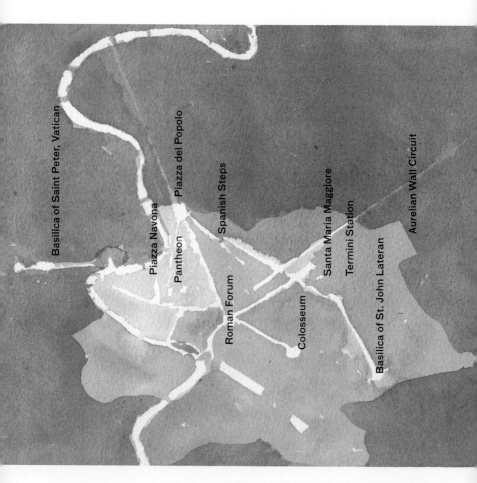

Sketch diagrammatic map of Rome showing the major features of the Tiber River, the Aurelian Wall (which contained the urban area up until the late 19th century), and the major axes of Baroque Rome (straight) and the 19th century and early 20th century new thoroughfares. The locations of major landmarks are indicated.

The Lay of the Land

Rome can be confusing to the first-time visitor. Its age and evolution over time deny it an orienting street grid, and its river, the Tiber, meanders like a writhing snake, and thus fails to provide any navigational assist. Getting around on public transportation (bus, tram and two metro lines) also takes more time to master than the length of the average visitor's sojourn, and travel by car or taxi is stymied by the many pedestrian-only streets in the *centro storico* (historic core). Walking then, is the most practical way to get around, with the occasional bus or taxi for longer trips out of the center. The best talismans to help memory and orientation are, first and foremost, the city's topography, consisting of its famous seven hills set upon the flat flood planes of the river valley. Next, consider these in relation to the city's growth from the center, and layered accretions of monuments, streets, and defensive walls from those early origins. One is almost constantly within sight of a famous monument, fountain, street, square or defensive wall, and as the visitor's memory map becomes populated with these recognizable signposts, the confusing jumble of history can be mastered and possessed.

Finally, while Rome's street pattern does not follow a typical orthogonal urban grid (with the exception of some of the late nineteenth century districts like Prati), there have been some exceptional and memorable streets and networks of axes created over time, and these can help in orientation. There was an attempt to impose some order on the jumble by Pope Sixtus V in the late sixteenth century, to create a capital whose image rose to the expectation for Rome as the center of Christendom. Sixtus conceived a system of connected processional axes linking nodal spaces throughout the city. In his short papacy, he was only able to implement one of the streets (via Sistina), but he did manage to relocate Egyptian obelisks to mark the centers of the Piazza del Popolo and Saint Peter's, while at St. John Lateran the obelisk marks the end of an important vista as one travels the via Merulana. These nodal points are today linked by straight axial streets, of which the so-called "Trident"—the three radial streets leading out of Piazza del Popolo to the south—are the most notable example. In the nineteenth century, as a response to the increase of vehicular traffic, a series of broad avenues were cut through the city. These include the via Nazionale and the Corso Vittorio Emanuele which form a swath across the city from the Termini Station to the Tiber. In the 1930s, Mussolini cut an additional network of boulevards through the ancient fora around the Capitoline Hill, in order to provide an easy means of vehicular access to the sea via his new city, the Espozizione Universale Roma (EUR). All of these monumental ways from three distinct periods should serve to orient the confused visitor.

Chapter 1.
Nonstraightforward Architecture:
A Gentle Manifesto

From its oxymoronic subtitle, juxtaposing elements that appear contradictory, Venturi announces a revisionist view of architecture. As a *manifesto*, his essay is in dramatic contrast to Le Corbusier's formulaic *Vers une architecture* of 1923, to which Vincent Scully compares it. The Venturi essay was so controversial that professors in many schools of architecture, including UCLA where Frederick Fisher was a graduate student, discouraged students from reading it. It was thought to open Pandora's box, inciting the wholesale abandonment of the rules of modernist design, and with arguments thought too subtle for students' grasp. Stephen Harby came to Yale having grown up in Cambridge in the shadow of Harvard's Graduate School of Design. Its dean, Walter Gropius, was a founder and champion of the International Style and represented the polar opposite of Venturi's world-view. Stephen found the work provocative when it was assigned to him by the very same Vincent Scully. Striking out against the purist orthodoxy of Modernism, Venturi championed, in his own words, an architecture which was..."hybrid...compromising ...distorted... ambiguous...perverse...boring...conventional...accommodating...redundant... vestigial...inconsistent and equivocal...messy vitality...non sequitur...duality." Venturi's book was and still is a breath of fresh intellectual air in the myopic discourse of architecture.

Chapter 2.
Complexity and Contradiction vs. Simplification and Picturesqueness

Venturi's juxtaposition of two radically different viewpoints is, in fact, a world-view. The stakes are higher than architectural style. To examine such a thesis is to open up to the real world, and the complex, layered world of Rome that no doubt confronted and influenced Venturi. His words refer to the mathematics of uncertainty, to a broader view of culture. While this chapter is general in scope, and no specific examples of Roman buildings are offered, it is informed in every way by what Venturi learned from Rome. He sets up the opposition of two world-views. On one side, he considers the quest to reduce and simplify human needs and functions, with the resulting architectural expression of the modern movement. On the other side, he contemplates the far more complex and messy reality of the world to which an architect must respond.

Rome is at once the eternal city, and a city layered in time. It presents a palimpsest of different periods, with multiple uses and functions for any given spot, and few instances of simplicity. One example (although not one cited by Venturi) of this layering of historical traces is evident in the Piazza Navona located in the Campus Martius. Its shape of a narrow rectangle with one semicircular end comes from its original use as a stadium—the stadium of emperor Domitian built in CE 92-96. The name "Navona" is a derivation of the word "Agone," which means contest. As the empire and its monuments crumbled into rubble, the abandoned stadium was taken over by squatters who gradually created places to dwell in its shell. Eventually, noble families were attracted to the square – the city's and Europe's grandest – and built their palaces there. One of these families, the Pamphilj, produced a pope, Innocent X (1644-66), and his dream was to transform the square and the family's palazzo along half of its west flank to a papal seat whose grandeur would surpass that of the Vatican across the Tiber. He set about commissioning great works by Borromini, Rainaldi and Bernini, which embellish the square to this day.

Chapter 3.
Ambiguity

In this chapter Venturi celebrates the possibilities suggested by the conjunction "or." For him, a delightful and titillating ambiguity arises when aspects or details of a building's design suggest alternative interpretations. As he does often throughout the book, he calls on contemporary literary criticism for support, celebrating the possibility of multiple interpretations when poetic or dramatic metaphors are not absolute. Venturi cites the work of literary theorist William Empson's *Seven Types of Ambiguity*, which presents Shakespeare's use of complexity of language and ambiguity of meaning as a deliberate device to enhance the dramatic telling of the story. He draws on three examples from Rome, two of papal association from the Mannerist and Baroque periods, and one secular post-war example:

> **1. Gianlorenzo Bernini, Façade, Palazzo di Propaganda Fide, Rome, 1644**
> **[Page 21, illustration 7]**
>
> These oscillating relationships, complex and contradictory, are the source of the ambiguity and tension characteristic to the medium of architecture. The conjunction "or" with a question mark can usually describe ambiguous relationships. ... (1) Bernini's pilasters on the Propaganda Fide: Are they positive pilasters or negative panel divisions? The (2) ornamental cove in the Casino Pio IV [the original text refers, in error to Pius V as the creator] at the Vatican is perverse: is it more wall or more vault? ... (3) Luigi Moretti's apartments on the Via Parioli in Rome: are they one building with a split or two buildings joined?

The Palazzo di Propaganda Fide faces the square in central Rome where the Spanish embassy is located. Thus the area, the adjacent square to the north and the grand flight of steps ascending the hill to the east, are all referred to as "Spanish" [Piazza di Spagna, Spanish Steps, etc.]. This large trapezoidal building fills its block, and was commissioned to house the functions related to missionary activities, literally, "propagation of the faith."

Venturi's delight in this façade focuses on the pilasters. Pilasters are an architectural element like columns, except rectangular and usually engaged or attached to the façade wall. He asks whether they are intended to be read positively, as applied pilasters, or as vestigial masses of the building after the intermediate panels (containing the windows) are carved away. Venturi does not comment on, and perhaps was not aware of, what we have always seen as the most interesting aspect of Bernini's design. That is, the pilasters are not vertical but lean inward very slightly from their bases as they rise up the façade. This is particularly noticeable when the sun is raking across the plane of the elevation in the afternoon, as shown in our illustration. The shadows cast by the pilasters appear deeper at the base than they are at the top. Venturi's illustration, an etching, does not show this, and the shadows are a consistent width all the way up. The design suggests that Bernini considered the pilasters part of the mass of the building rather than applied elements. In typical masonry construction, and as often seen in fortified walls, the wall is thicker at the base, providing optimal strength and stability. This would support Venturi's alternate interpretation, that the three intermediate panels are in fact carved into the mass and the face of the pilasters represent the original outer surface.

In addition, we encounter one of the many symbols found throughout Rome and often placed above an important entrance, the coat of arms on a shield. Most often the symbol is a papal crest, signified by papal regalia, crossed keys, and a tall papal hat resembling a beehive. This shield also depicts actual sculptural bees, the symbol of the Barberini family, whose pope, Urban VIII, commissioned this building. As you tour Rome, be on the lookout for symbols of the great families of Rome (fleur de lis=Farnese, mounds=Chigi, balls=Medici, etc.), clues to when the building was built and by whom.

Venturi will refer to this building twice more, to the interior and to a façade around the corner where a chapel and other changes to the existing Bernini-designed building involve designs by Francesco Borromini. These two architects, were, along with Carlo Maderno, Carlo Rainaldi, and Pietro da Cortona, the leaders of high Baroque design in seventeenth century Rome. They were contemporaries, formed as apprentices in the studio of Maderno, and they were highly competitive. Though unmentioned by Venturi, the fact that Borromini was called in to replace existing parts of the building designed by Bernini would have been a politically fraught situation that gave rise to its own form of ambiguity as to their respective roles and responsibilities.

2. Ligorio, Casino di Pio IV, Vatican, Rome (1562) [Page 20, illustration 8]

The Casino of Pius IV, located in the Vatican gardens behind the Basilica of San Pietro, presently houses the Pontifical Academy of Sciences. Permission is required for access. This jewel-like garden pavilion was begun by Pope Paul IV in 1558 and completed with designs of Pirro Ligorio in 1562 by the next pope, Pius IV. The design is inspired by Hadrian's Villa, with which Ligorio was familiar, having conducted excavations there and having designed the nearby Vill d'Este at Tivoli. Ornate plaster stucco and frescoed decoration, inspired by examples found in Roman antiquity, encrusts most exterior and interior surfaces. The decorations were the work of Federico Barocci, Federico Zuccari, and Santi di Tito, based on imagery from mythology and biblical scenes.

1. Gianlorenzo Bernini, Façade, Palazzo di Propaganda Fide, Rome, 1644
[Page 21, illustration 7]

2. Ligorio, Casino di Pio IV, Vatican, Rome (1562) [Page 20, illustration 8]

It delighted Venturi that a flat palazzo wall in a vertical plane is instead represented as part of the curved ceiling vault. There are many other aspects of ambiguity in this complex and interesting work in the Post-Renaissance style known as *Mannerism*. Many things are not what they might at first appear to be, or what convention would dictate they *should* be. The pavilion was commissioned at the height of the Counter-Reformation movement, when the emphasis was on a return to focused piety and devout religious observance. Why, then, would it be deemed appropriate to create a place for the enjoyment of earthly delights, in a garden adorned with symbols and themes from pagan mythology?

3. Luigi Moretti, Apartment Building (Casa Girasole), via Parioli (actually viale Bruno Bozzi, 64), Rome (1947-50) [Page 22, illustration 10]

This small apartment building was designed and built after World War II in the luxurious and growing residential district of Parioli. The name, *girasole*, is Italian for *sunflower* and refers to the angled bay windows on the sides, configured to fan outward to maximize solar exposure like a flower following the sun.

The prolific Moretti designed important buildings in the Fascist era, including an exquisitely detailed private gymnasium for Mussolini, and he continued to practice through 1971, including his Watergate Apartments in Washington DC. One wonders if the broken pediment of Casa Girasole was the inspiration for the Vanna Venturi house of 1964, under design when Venturi was writing *Complexity and Contradiction*?

Like all arts, architecture has linguistic properties. Within each language (Classicism, Modernism, Post Modernism, etc.) there are words and syntax understood by a community. In architecture, the words are elements such as walls, windows, and roofs. And architectural syntax is the way in which elements are assembled. Venturi was acutely interested in the linguistic dimension of architecture and his fondness for the Mannerist and Baroque periods may have stemmed from the rich application of linguistic irony. He applied linguistic analysis to work that wasn't associated with this approach and may not have been conceived with this dimension in mind. In particular, he exposed the supposed rationality of Modernism as having the same kind of rhetorical intentions as the Classical language disdained by Modernists as superficial. He embraced this rhetorical approach in his own practice, to the consternation of much of the profession at the time.

Moretti's highly sophisticated building abounds in rhetorical misdirection (or the use of familiar elements in unconventional ways) in form, organization, and materiality. The façade in conventional use would provide a strong boundary between exterior and interior, to be penetrated through an entry doorway, marking the transition from outside to inside. Here it is split in the middle, creating a slot, which allows the exterior to penetrate deep into the building, dividing it into two lobes on either side to reflect the floor plan of two flanking apartments. This allows light and air to penetrate deep into what would normally be the dark core of the building. The same façade extends beyond the block of the building mass at each corner, creating an ambiguity in the way the solid building mass is perceived. Is it a block or is it a peeled skin? The symmetry of the building, so clearly expressed by the front elevation with its central slot, is contradicted by the placement of the stair off center to the left and by the fact that at the top of the central opening the upper parts of the split gable do not align from side to side. Finally, in a nod to the Renaissance palazzo's conventional use of a heavily rusticated base with rough hewn large blocks of masonry, here Moretti uses the rough masonry, but uses it as an appliqué like wallpaper revealing the thinness of the stone. All of these contradictions and ambiguities are examples of rhetorical misdirection.

Contemplating Bernini's pilasters as something of relevance in the late 20th century was strange enough. Comparing them to a little known (in the US) mid-century Italian architect who on earlier projects had worked for Mussolini under the rubric of "ambiguity" was startling, and yet exciting. Everything becomes relevant in Venturi's universe, including unimportant and even "bad" architecture.

3. Luigi Moretti, Apartment Building (Casa Girasole), via Parioli (actually viale Bruno Bozzi, 64), Rome (1947-50) [Page 22, illustration 10]

Chapter 4.
Contradictory Levels: The Phenomenon of "Both-And" in Architecture

While the examples in the last chapter required us to choose among competing readings, here Venturi celebrates the richness implicit in multivalent readings and the possibility that an architectural element or expression can say one thing while at the same time it means or suggests another. The difference is that here, both readings are possible at the same time. Pilasters in the *Propaganda Fide* are either pilasters or wall; the stylized, originally planar, wall elevations draped over the curved vaults of the Casino of Pius IV are no longer flat. However, the example of Moretti's *Casa Girasole*, with which he concludes the last chapter, presages this one. The bifurcated gable, does in fact still read as a unified building façade, and at the same time it suggests two separate structures.

> **4. Michelangelo, Rear Façade, St. Peter's, Rome (1546-93)**
> **[Page 25, illustration 19]**
>
> Michelangelo's enormous rectangular openings in the attic story of the rear facade of St. Peter's are wider than they are tall, so they must be spanned the long way. This is perverse in relation to the spanning limitations of masonry, which dictate in classical architecture that big openings, such as these, be vertically proportioned. Because one usually expects vertical proportions, the longitudinal span expresses relative smallness.

In order to observe what Venturi describes, it will be necessary to gain access to the papal gardens to the rear of St. Peters, on a tour offered regularly by the Vatican Museums. These massive elevations are the result of Michelangelo's revisions to the centralized plan of St. Peter's Basilica. It was originally designed by Donato Bramante in 1506, a half century earlier, itself a radical departure from the existing five-aisled early Christian basilica dating from 315-349. When Bramante died in 1514, construction was only partially complete and would be largely replaced, even though Bramante's central plan and large dome, based on the Pantheon, would remain to inspire his successors.

Michelangelo followed in the footsteps of most of Bramante's pupils who tinkered with the master's design throughout the early sixteenth century. Michelangelo's contribution is a clarification and simplification of the plan, maintaining its centric geometry of central dome flanked by four domical side chapels at the four corners. He greatly thickened the exterior walls and piers supporting the huge dome and modified the profile of the dome. The portion of the façade we are looking at is the curved section that occurs at either the apse or the two transept ends. Like everything in St. Peter's, the scale of this elevation is immense, and Venturi makes the point with a subsequent citation of the same façade in Chapter 8.

4. Michelangelo, Rear Façade, St. Peter's, Rome (1546-93) [Page 25, illustration 19]

It is hard to know exactly what Michelangelo's intentions were with the horizontal openings in the attic that delight Venturi, but it seems likely to involve the composition of the façade. Shadows cast by the architectural trim and dark voids of the openings are key elements in the dramatic expression of this composition. James Ackerman, the great architectural historian, presents this interpretation in his definitive monograph on Michelangelo:

> *After completing the dome model, Michelangelo in his last years turned to the design of the attic, where he achieved the same balance of force and repose. He may have made no decisive designs before this time since the model was built without an attic facing, but the construction of the apertures implies that he had intended to give the window frames a vertical axis. In the revised design, the apertures were covered by horizontal frames, which help to inhibit the vertical surge. The new accent was to have been reinforced by a continuous balustrade.[3]*

Modernist design theory would oppose abandoning rules of convention while merely striving for visual effect in the design of a façade, and this no doubt explains Venturi's celebration of it.

5. Bernini, Sant' Andrea al Quirinale, Rome (1658-70) [P. 26, illustration 24]

The basilica, which has a mono-directional space, and the central-type church, which has omnidirectional space, represent alternating traditions in Western church plans. But another tradition has accommodated churches which are both-and, in answer to spatial, structural, programmatic, and symbolic needs. The Mannerist elliptical plan of the sixteenth century is both central and directional. It's culmination is Bernini's Sant' Andrea al Quirinale, whose main directional axis contradictorily spans the short axis. Nikolaus Pevsner has shown how pilasters rather than open chapels bisect both ends of the transverse axis of the sidewalls, thereby reinforcing the short axis toward the altar.

Interestingly enough, this church was commissioned by the Jesuit order, which rarely used circular or elliptical plans, preferring the longitudinal plan. The move to turn the long axis perpendicular to the path of movement may have been intended to heighten the sense of drama. Immediately after entering the church, one is confronted by the high altar chapel and the broken pediment that surmounts it and supports the image of Sant' Andrea going heavenward, repeating the same image depicted in the painting below. The elements of painting, sculpture, and architecture coalesce in a dramatic narrative synthesis in the depiction of *The Apotheosis of St. Andrew*.

---

3 James S. Ackerman, *The Architecture of Michelangelo*, London: A. Zwemmer, Ltd., 1961, p. 100.

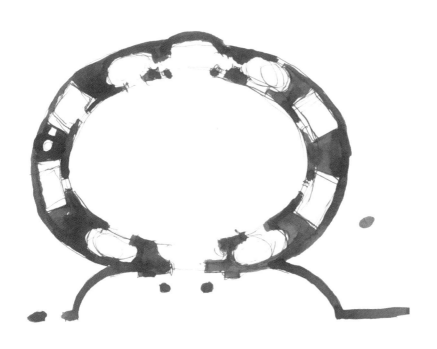

5. Bernini, Sant' Andrea al Quirinale, Rome (1658-70) [P. 26, illustration 24]

5. Bernini, Sant' Andrea al Quirinale, Rome (1658-70) [P. 26, illustration 24]
Interior View

6. Borromini, Church of the Re Magi, Palazzo di Propaganda Fide, Rome (1646-66) [p. 27, illustration 25]

6. Borromini, Church of the Re Magi, Palazzo di Propaganda Fide, Rome (1646-66) [p. 27, illustration 25]

Borromini's chapel in the Propoganda Fide is a directional hall in plan, but its alternating bays counteract this effect: a large bay dominates the small end; a small bay bisects the center of the long wall. The rounded corners, as well, begin to imply a continuity of enclosure and a central type plan. (These characteristics occur in the courtyard of San Carlo alle Quatttro Fontane too.) And the diagonal grid-like ribs in the ceiling indicate a multidirectional structure as much like a dome as a vault.

Here we return to the building complex mentioned (1) in the context of the façade designed by Bernini two years earlier, and this is the chapel which replaced Bernini's construction. One of the challenges Borromini faced in the design of the chapel was the fact that it had to be embedded within the existing block of the building and needed to conform to existing fenestration. Borromini's use of a skeletal grid rather than planar walls and ceilings to envelop the space provides a zone of layered space around all sides and above. In this way, light filters in, not only through the differently spaced windows on the street side but also by means of skylights on the other side. This creates the impression that the chapel is freestanding rather than embedded in a building block.

7. Borromini, Palazzo di Propaganda Fide, Rome (1646-66) [P. 29, illustration 33]

In some rooms of the Palazzo di Propaganda Fide a straddling arch in the corners allows the space to be rectangular below and continuous above. This is similar to Wren's ceiling configuration in St. Stephen's Walbrook.

The Mannerist and Baroque periods delighted Venturi, and he illuminated the sophisticated formal and rhetorical play of his favorites, Michelangelo, Bernini and Borromini. His analytical presentations give the reader powerful tools of expression and interpretation that are applicable in all the arts. Here he is celebrating the superimposition of a rounded form upon a rectangular plan, and it is the columns, in the case of the Wren example, or the configuration of the pilasters here that form the transition between the two contrasting shapes. This is achieved by a sophisticated placement of the arch spring-points that are regular and logical with respect to both shapes. In this small room on the second level of the Palazzo Propaganda Fide the zone of primary interest is where the eight equal arches form the transition between walls and dome.

7. Borromini, Palazzo di Propaganda Fide, Rome (1646-66) [P. 29, illustration 33]

8. Borromini, San Carlo alle Quattro Fontane, Rome (1638-41)
[P. 27 illustrations 26 and 27]

Borromini's San Carlo alle Quatro Fontane abounds in ambiguous manifestations of both-and. The almost equal treatment of the four wings implied in the plan suggests a Greek cross, but the wings are distorted toward a dominant east-west axis, thus suggesting a Latin cross, while the fluid continuity of the walls indicates a distorted circular plan. Rudolf Wittkower has analyzed similar contradictions in section. The pattern of the ceiling in the articulations of its complex mouldings suggests a dome on pendentives over the crossing of a Greek cross. The shape of the ceiling in its overall continuity distorts these elements into parodies of themselves, and suggests rather a dome generated from an undulating wall. These distorted elements are both continuous and articulated.

Here we find ourselves in one of the greatest and most sophisticated works of the high Baroque, highly admired and analyzed by architects and scholars of all stripes. We tell our students that upon entering this space, before they start to take photographs or, preferably, to sketch, they should sit down and spend a few minutes observing everything they can. The plan, which is mirrored in a crypt below of somewhat simpler configuration, is underpinned by a simple but sophisticated geometric construction derived from two back-to-back equilateral triangles. They determine the radii that describe the compound curves of the plan of the oval dome and the concave chapels on the two cross axes. One can also imagine an underlying structure of a circular plan with regularly spaced columns that support a hemispherical dome. Recall, once again, the Pantheon or the Jefferson Memorial in Washington, DC. The space has been squeezed at four points along diagonal axes, producing a deformed shape described by the entablatures the columns support. Four straight segments are interspersed by round shapes that define the ends of the orthogonal axes.

Another curious instance of "both and," a highly original detail, can be observed in the arches that surmount the four large curved spaces at altar, entry bay and side chapels, most notably on the sides. Observe the flat surfaces of the arches that occur just below and within the surrounding stepped fasciae in the architrave. The first expresses the face of the arch, while the next surface, roughly 90 °, is the underside of the arch. Tracing this surface up the apex of the arch, it twists around and becomes the underside facing down, while the adjacent plane also twists around to become the rear of the arch. These are but two of the multivalent elements in this complex and exquisite architectural gem.

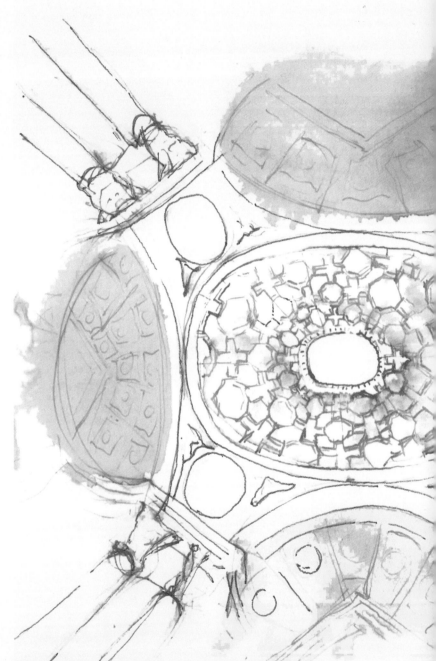

8. Borromini, San Carlo alle Quattro Fontane, Rome (1638-41)
[P. 27 illustrations 26 and 27]
Left: The watercolor plan
Right: The sketch plan

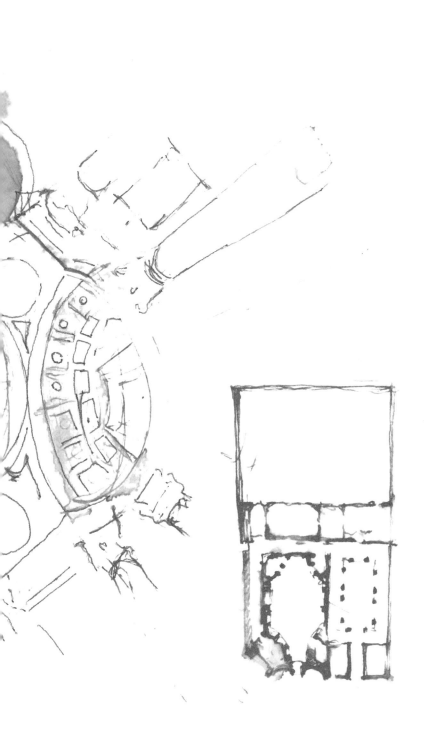

Interior view looking up

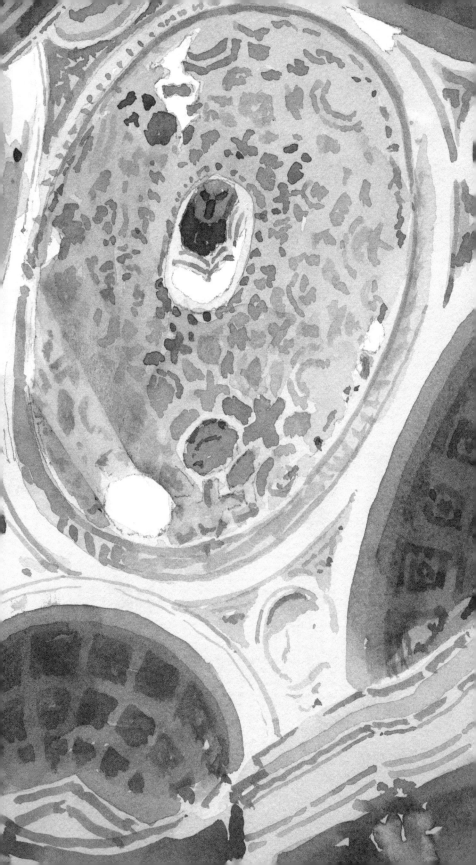

Chapter 5.
Contradictory Levels Continued: The Double-Functioning Element

In this chapter, Venturi confronts one of the sacred tenets of modernism, the belief that every architectural form and element should be the truthful expression of a singular and pure function. Buildings and their component rooms should be organized to reflect discreet and individual functions in each space, and the building components of enclosure and surface should be uniform and consistent. The oft repeated phrase, "form follows function" that became the battle cry of the modern movement, was coined in a slightly different form by American architect Louis Sullivan in his 1896 article, "The Tall Office Building Artistically Considered."[4]

> **9. S. Maria in Cosmedin, Rome, (c. 780, 1120-23) P. 35, illustration 45]**
> In S. Maria in Cosmedin's nave the column form results from its dominant, precise function as a point support...But the alternating piers in the same nave are intrinsically double functioning. They enclose and direct space as much as they support structure.

This church, at the site of one of the earliest spots of settlement in ancient Rome, the Foro Boario (cattle market), dates from the eighth century and was expanded in the twelfth. It is a prime example of the messy and complex process of layering and reusing existing forms—both in plan and in vertical section—that so inspired Venturi's work. The church was built on the site of a pre-Christian temple of Hercules, of which the altar is still visible in the crypt. It was also previously the site of a 6th Century diaconia, or Christian welfare center. At the ground level it incorporates the columns of a Roman imperial building, still visible in the wall behind the entrance, as well as the lateral walls. The other columns which comprise the two arcades of the nave, and to which Venturi refers, are *spolia*—pieces reused from older buildings, in this case Roman. This is obvious from the fact they are mismatched. Another reused element is the circular stone bearing the image of a man's face, usually identified as the god Oceanus, complete with gaping mouth, mounted on the end wall at the left end of the porch. This is the famous "bocca della verita" in which Audrey Hepburn placed her hand in the film, *Roman Holiday* as proof that she was telling the truth. Today there will be lines of tourists waiting for their turn! Alternating rows of columns interspersed by solid masonry piers that extend the wall plane to the ground were relatively common in early Christian architecture, and can often be seen in cloisters. They add

---

4   Sullivan, Louis H. (1896). "The Tall Office Building Artistically Considered." *Lippincott's Magazine* (March 1896): 403–409.

stiffness and structural stability, which would not have been possible with columns alone.

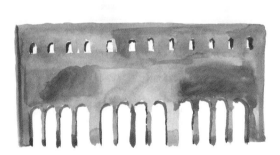

9. S. Maria in Cosmedin, Rome, (c. 780, 1120-23) P. 35, illustration 45]
Top image: Perspective of choir screen crossing nave colonnade.

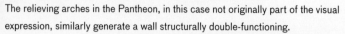

10. Pantheon, Rome Perspective [P. 35, illustration 49]

The relieving arches in the Pantheon, in this case not originally part of the visual expression, similarly generate a wall structurally double-functioning.

This is one of Venturi's purposeful misreadings of a building to make a point. He turns an engineering device into an unrelated rhetorical one, never intended by the builders. As he states, these arches would not have been noticed by the early second century observer of what must have been a truly revolutionary building. The experience of visiting the Pantheon in its Roman context would have been astonishing and surprising, and freighted with no small amount of ambiguity and contradiction. Our understanding of the original urban context of the Pantheon comes from a variety of sources, both contemporary from the time and more recent. In the 1930s Mussolini commissioned a large plaster scale model that depicts the city as it was in the time of Constantine (approximately 312 ce). The model was based on excavations, the fragmentary marble plan (from antiquity), and a range of other sources. It shows a Pantheon tightly embedded and hemmed in by other structures on the sides and in the rear, with a large rectangular open piazza in front, about twice the depth of the present Piazza della Rotonda and enclosed with porticos on three sides. The viewer would approach the building from this side and would perceive the front porch with eight monolithic granite columns supporting a triangular pediment. Furthermore, it was thought that this pediment was designed to be higher, which would have obscured more of the drum behind, but was lowered during construction.[5] Such a prospect, resembling the many Greek style temples throughout the city, would not be out of the ordinary. Viewers would not be aware of the large cylindrical drum behind this façade, as we are today, and upon passing through the portico and penetrating the interior, they would have been awestruck. They would have been immersed in a unique spatial experience never seen before on this scale. This of course is what makes the Pantheon one of the world's most significant buildings, the culmination of technological and structural innovation. The new materials of brick and concrete are employed in brilliant technological and proportional harmony to make possible a dome, which to this day is one of the largest spans in the world. The exterior relieving arches, noted by Venturi, are part of the structural innovation of this amazing building.

The function of the Pantheon is enigmatic, as is the date of its construction. We are given a false clue in the inscription in the pediment that refers to a Roman functionary Agrippa, dating to 27 CE. However, it is established from dates on brick stamps found throughout the structure that the date-range of construction is a century later, 118 to 128 CE. The reason this building

---

5   See Mark Wilson Jones.

10. Pantheon, Rome Perspective [P. 35, illustration 49]

is considered one of the most perfect, harmonious and significant in all the world and in all eras, has to do with the meaning expressed through its geometry and its sole source of light, introduced through the central oculus at the apex of the dome. The interior consists of a circular drum supporting a hemispherical coffered dome. The height of the drum equals the radius of the dome, and thus when the hemispherical dome is completed to become a sphere it intersects with the floor. How perfect is that? The drum is punctuated by a series of openings distributed around its perimeter. These vary in scale and importance depending on whether they are on the major cross axes (4 openings with apsidal ends), the secondary diagonal axes (4 openings with rectangular side spaces), or finally the tabernacles which mark eight more axes of lesser importance. This hierarchical "weighting" of the sixteen radial axes is further reinforced by the configuration of the 28 coffer bays in the dome. The four orthogonal axes bisect them, the next four axes on the 45° angle align with a rib, and there is no correlation with the other radials. The floor is marked off by a Cartesian or square grid as opposed to the radial organization of what rises above the earth. This could have been intended by the builders to create a distinction between the earth we inhabit and where we spend our quotidian lives, as opposed to the celestial realm of the heavens overhead to which we might aspire. The floor is not flat, but curves gently away from the center, further reinforcing the impression that we are standing on this earth with its curved surface peering into the heavens above.

When we consider the lighting of the Pantheon, this distinction between the earthly and celestial realms is even more distinct. The interior is bathed in natural light, which is primarily introduced through the open oculus, whose area is only four percent of that of the floor. The quality of light varies depending on the weather and the season. When sunny, the passing of each day is marked by the journey of the projected disc of the sun as it travels down from the top of dome and back again as the earth turns from sunrise to sunset, and across the dome and walls as it moves from east to west. The positioning of the sun as the earth tilts on its axis according to the seasons is also marked by how deep into the space the sun disc travels. In winter, it only reaches the mid-point of the coffered dome, while at noon on June 21 – the summer solstice – a large bright circle of light bathes the floor directly in front of the main entrance. Could this have been intended to highlight a colossal statue, possibly of Hadrian, the building's patron? Thus the building becomes a celestial astronomical instrument like a giant sundial that tells us the time of day and the season.

Yet another distinction of this remarkable structure is the fact that it is one of very few where most of the original surfaces are preserved intact from the time of its construction at the height of the Roman Empire. Thus we can admire rare and precious materials (porphyry from Egypt, giallo antico marble

Interior view

from Tunisia, verde antiqua from Egypt, etc.) that speak of the power and extent of the empire in the early second century all across the Mediterranean. Its preservation is the result of its near continuous use to our day, becoming a place of Christian worship in 609. Its fame has also meant that it serves as the prototype for domed structures all over the world, of which Jefferson's Library at the University of Virginia and the Jefferson Memorial on the Potomac by John Russell Pope in Washington, DC are but two.

> ### 11. Borromini, S. Maria dei Sette Dolori [P. 38, Illustration 53]
>
> The double functioning element can be a detail. Mannerist and Baroque Buildings abound in drip mouldings which become sills, windows which become niches, cornice ornaments which accommodate windows, quoin strips which are also pilasters, and architraves which make arches.

This convent, whose exterior façade was never completed, built between 1642 and 1655, is located on via Garibaldi in Trastevere at the base of the Gianicolo hill. It is now part of the luxurious Donna Savelli Hotel and should be accessible during daytime hours. Before entering the main sanctuary described by Venturi, one passes through a vestibule, whose cruciform plan terminates in concave apses alternating with convex sides, and may have been inspired by similarly configured spaces at Hadrian's Villa. In the main sanctuary, the entablature resting on the columns, transitions directly from a lintel to an arch. Also at Hadrian's villa a similar detail is used in the arcade that surrounds the so-called Scenic Canal. It is possible that, without acknowledging it, Venturi – in these several mentions of unconventional uses of the elements of the classical orders – is celebrating the fact that in the hands of Borromini and many other architects, classical language is a living, fluid thing, and not the dead language that Venturi's modernist contemporaries would have considered it.

> ### 12. Borromini, Palazzo di Propaganda Fide, Rome [P. 38, illustration 55]
>
> Borromini's mouldings in the rear facades of the Propaganda Fide are both window frames and pediments.

Of interest here is another example of the double functioning element, which in this case is the frame of the window. At the apex it is given a gable form, mirroring the pediment above. In the conventional treatment of the palazzo window surround in the Renaissance and Baroque periods, the window would be given a rectangular frame. Above it, and separated from it by a flat panel, would be a triangular pediment. Borromini, always inclined to invent novel expressions derived from the familiar elements of classical expression, here combines the two elements of window frame and pediment.

11. Borromini, S. Maria dei Sette Dolori [P. 38, Illustration 53]

Opposite Page: 12. Borromini, Palazzo di Propaganda Fide, Rome
[P. 38, illustration 55]

Chapter 6.
Accommodation and the Limitations of Order: The Conventional Element

This crucial chapter can be summed up, "Our buildings must survive the cigarette machine." In it, Venturi discusses the inevitable clutter of modern life as it intervenes to disrupt the systems of order that the prototypical architect seeks to impose. The following reference to *spolia*, or the reuse of elements of prior buildings, should educate our eye to this phenomenon, so prevalent in Rome:

> *The value of such contradictory meanings has been acknowledged in both evolutionary and revolutionary architecture—from the collages of fragments of post-Roman architecture, the so-called Spolium architecture in which column capitals are used as bases, for instance, to the Renaissance style itself, where the old Classical Roman vocabulary was employed in new combinations. And James Ackerman has described Michelangelo as "rarely adopting a motif [in his architecture] without giving it a new form or a new meaning. Yet he invariably retained essential features from ancient models in order to force the observer to recollect the source while enjoying the innovations."*

This passage summarizes as well as any other the role Rome and its layered, messy, jumble has had in informing Venturi's thinking about architecture.

Chapter 7.
Contradiction Adapted

This chapter celebrates instances where existing conditions contradict the conventional and pure order of a design system such as façade organization or a structural grid—the "disintegration of a prototype." Venturi writes, "A vivid play of order and the circumstantial is, in fact, a characteristic of all Italian architecture, with its bold contradictions of monumentality and expediency."

> **13. Peruzzi, Palazzo Massimo, Rome [P. 45, illustration 66]**
> In the Palazzo Massimo a curving rather than an angular distortion accommodated the façade to the street, which also curved before it was changed in the nineteenth century.

Palazzo Massimo alle Colonne, designed by Baldassare Peruzzi is one of two, built side-by-side for two brothers, in this case, Pietro Massimo. Its companion, designed by Giovanni Mangone is the more understated palace immediately to its left, for Angelo Massimo. Palazzo Massimo alle Colonne remains in the hands of the original family, and its interior is only open to the public once a year on March 16, when a festival commemorates events on that day in 1583. St. Philip Neri performed a miracle bringing back to momentary life 14 year old Paolo Massimo, who suffered from a fatal illness. The commission was the result of the severe damage to previous palaces on the site during the sack of Rome by the troops of Charles V, Holy Roman Emperor in 1527. The curved façade, whose plan comprises a circular arc in the center flanked by two straight tangents on either side is the unique and distinguishing feature of this beautiful composition. This feature makes it a prime example of Mannerism, or the deliberate departure from the conventional classical rules of design formulated in the Renaissance. Of course, it is to be expected that a palace would take the form of a rectangular block and that its façade would be a flat plane. Instead, this curving façade has the quality of a bent piece of leather, and the fact that Peruzzi has floated the upper story windows on this curving surface without the use of more conventional vertical pilasters and horizontal string-courses, heightens this effect.

The original context of the palace was a very narrow, curving lane, and not the broad traffic-choked boulevard that confronts us today; the latter was laid out in the nineteenth century when wheeled vehicles replaced foot traffic. The curvature of the façade and perhaps the street as well probably took their cue from an ancient Roman semi-circular Odeon or small theater that was part of the stadium complex of Domitian. This stadium has also given form to nearby Piazza Navona. One would have perceived the façade in two

Façade View

ways in this original context. First, walking along the narrow lane, one would have seen the two straight segments on either side obliquely, and then once in front of the building, the deep dark spaces of the porch between the six, free-standing Tuscan columns would have gestured to the entrance. This central curved portion of the façade is also aligned on the center of via del Paradiso, the perpendicular street opposite, a likely route of approach. Thus the façade is symmetrical even though the accompanying image Venturi and we use to illustrate it is only possible with the long view enabled by the widening of the street. The symmetrical façade, which would suggest a typical symmetrical plan arrangement, in this case is completely misleading and contradictory to the actual plan, which presents a skewed axis progressing through entry portico, corridor, first courtyard, portico and rear courtyard, with the block of the palazzo, the courtyard and the major spaces asymmetrically arranged.

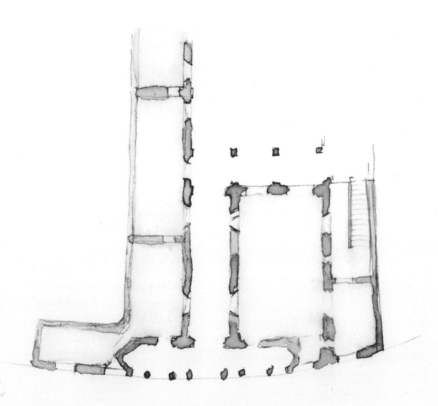

13. Peruzzi, Palazzo Massimo, Rome [P. 45, illustration 66]

Chapter 8.
Contradiction Juxtaposed

In Venturi's words, here we have progressed from "the kid glove treatment, in contradiction juxtaposed" to the "shock treatment" where elements starkly jarring in scale and character are introduced.

> **14. Michelangelo [in fact Jacopo Barozzi da Vignola, and Giacomo della Porta], Rear Façade, Palazzo Farnese [P. 57, Illustration 94]**
> It is the texture of Mannerist rustication which clashes in the same way when it abuts the precise detail of the classical orders in a Renaissance façade. But Michelangelo's [actually Della Porta's] loggia in the center of the upper floor of the rear façade of the Palazzo Farnese in relation to the walls adjacent to it reflects a more ambiguous kind of contradiction. Giacomo della Porta's exceptional central elements on the floor below—pilasters, arches and architrave—vary only slightly in rhythm and not at all in scale, and the transition from the typical window bays on each side to the middle bays is consistent in detail and scale. The openings of Michelangelo's loggia above are violently contrasting in scale and rhythm with the typical elements to the sides as well as in the higher floor elevation which they imply. The pilasters also, because of their elevation and height, violently break the frieze below the cornice, and the cornice itself recedes rather than advances to match the projections and boldness of the elements below it. The scale of this cornice is smaller because of the increased rhythm of the modillions, yet the modillions themselves (lions' heads) are identical to those on the other cornice and the mouldings are continuous throughout. Similarly ambiguous combinations of contradictions both juxtaposed and adapted, occur in the intermediate bays within the niche.

The Palazzo Farnese is among the grandest and most important high Renaissance palaces in Rome, the home of Cardinal Alessandro Farnese, who was elected Pope Paul III in 1534. A second Cardinal Alessandro Farnese, the Pope's grandson, also resided here for over 40 years, although as Vice Cancelliere, his official residence was the nearby Palazzo della Cancelleria. It was initially designed by Antonio da Sangallo the Younger in 1517, and expanded upon the papal election with designs by Michelangelo, Jacopo Barozzi da Vignola, and Giacomo della Porta. (The latter two were responsible for the upper two loggias, not Michelangelo, as Venturi states, but this doesn't impact the validity of his observations.) Its regular cube-like form, visible on all sides and set within a grand forecourt, is in direct contrast to the Palazzo Massimo of roughly the same period. Today, the palace houses the French embassy. The splendid interiors, including a magnificent grand hall with ceiling frescos by Annibale Caracci, can be visited by prior reservation or during the annual "open days" for French public buildings on September 18th and 19th.

14. Michelangelo [in fact Jacopo Barozzi da Vignola, and Giacomo della Porta] , Rear Façade, Palazzo Farnese [P. 57, Illustration 94]

15. Bramante, Belvedere Court, Vatican [P. 61, Illustration 106]

This enormous project consists of two long, sloping enfilades that border a series of stepped courts linking the Vatican palace with the Villa Belvedere, located on a promontory at the northern edge of the fortified walls of the Vatican enclave. Originally the court was open from one end to another with three terraces at different elevations, with changes in grade accommodated by flights of double stairs. It was inspired by the Roman Temple of Fortuna Primigenia in Palestrina, and following Bramante's revival of this motif, it became commonly used again. Two transverse wings have been introduced in the space, one housing the Vatican Library added by Pope Sixtus V in the sixteenth century, and the other, the Braccio Nuovo, a gallery for sculpture added in the nineteenth century. They transform what even today would be a magnificently grand space without precedent.

The layering that Venturi refers to is the superimposition of a trabeated (rectangular) structure on top of a row of arcuated (arched) openings. These are today filled in with a rusticated wall that originally would have been an open arcade. The concept of combining these two structural systems within one elevation comes from the Colosseum, although Alberti was the first to revive its use in the Renaissance in his design for the Palazzo Ruccelai in Florence of 1452-1458. Bramante, who came to Rome from Milan in 1499, was among the first architects of the Renaissance to consciously revive the forms and details of classical antiquity. Each of his other works of the same period drew on a key prototypical ancient Roman source. The cloister at Santa Maria della Pace (1500-1504) also uses the motif of arch within a rectangular frame, while the Tempietto at San Pietro in Montorio (1503) draws on the ancient Greek Tholos—or round tomb structure—to commemorate the supposed place of the martyrdom of St. Peter. The choir (1503-1509) at the apse of the church of Santa Maria del Popolo uses a bold barrel vault and deep coffering similar to that of either the Pantheon or the Basilica of Maxentius to return a sense of massiveness and *gravitas* to architectural expression. And of course, Bramante's design for the basilica of St. Peter (1506-1514) at the same time as the Belvedere Court, draws directly on the Pantheon for its inspiration. Many of these great projects were under the direct patronage and support of Pope Julius II, a great admirer of the classical. In February of 1506, the discovery of the sculpture of *Laocoön and his sons* in a vineyard near Santa Maria Maggiore caused him great excitement, and by March it was on display in a niche in the Belvedere Court. The statue is considered the greatest exemplar of classical perfection and expression of human suffering in art. It can be seen in the Octagonal courtyard of the Pio-Clementine museum, adjacent to this space.

16. Michelangelo, Porta Pia [P. 62-63, Illustrations 110 and 111],

The diverse structural elements that surround the great door in the Porta Pia are superimposed for ornament as well as structure. It abounds in redundant and rhetorical superadjacencies of a kind of ornament that is "about" structure. The vulnerable edges of the opening are protected by rusticated trim at the sides. Superimposed on the trim are pilasters that further define the sides of the door and support, together with the scrolled brackets above, the heavy complex of the pediment. This important opening is made eventful in the bearing wall by additional juxtapositions. The diagonal pediment protects the rectangular inscription block and the inverse segment of the sculptural garland which, in turn, plays against the curve of the semicircular relieving arch. The arch is at the head of a series of redundant structural spanning elements, including the horizontal lintel, which in turn relieves the flat arch, which is a continuation of the rusticated trim. Brackets or corbelling, which decrease the span, are suggested by the diagonals of the top corners of the opening. The exaggerated keystone is superimposed on the flat arch, the lintel and the tympanum of the arch.

In their complex relationships these elements are in varying degrees both structural and ornamental, frequently redundant, and sometimes vestigial. In the almost equal combination of horizontal, vertical, diagonal, and curve, they correspond to Sullivan's violently superimposed frames around the bull's-eye window of the boxlike Merchants' National Bank in Grinnell, Iowa.

It is appropriate that Michelangelo's Porta Pia is on the cover of the later 1977 edition of *Complexity and Contradiction*. Not only is Michelangelo Venturi's hero, but Porta Pia is a tour de force of architectural rhetoric divorced from function. What could be a more blatant challenge to Modern architecture? The early twentieth century British architect, Edwin Lutyens, another of Venturi's heroes and referenced in the very next example, referred to the "High game of Classicism" and nowhere is this more the case than in this virtuosic display of the use of the canonical elements simply for the fun of it.

16. Michelangelo, Porta Pia [P. 62-63, Illustrations 110 and 111],

17. Colossal head of Constantine, Court, Capitoline Museum [P. 67, Illustration 126]

18. Michelangelo, Rear Façade, St. Peter's. [P. 67, Illustration 128]

In Modern architecture contradictory juxtapositions of scale involving immediately adjacent elements are even rarer than superadjacencies. Such a manipulation of scale is seen in the accidental collage of the colossal head of Constantine and the louvered shutters in the courtyard of the Capitoline Museum. Significantly, it is usually in non-architectural configurations [illustration of a smokestack, Cunard Line ship] that such contrasts in scale occur today. In another context I have referred to the adjacencies of giant and minor orders in Mannerist and Baroque architecture. In the rear facade of St. Peter's, Michelangelo makes an even more contradictory contrast in scale: a blank window is juxtaposed with a capital bigger than the window itself.

Fifty years later, the colossal head of Constantine is still in the same spot, but the shuttered windows that so intrigued Venturi are gone, and the bases with their figures in sculptural relief have been relocated to the opposite side of the court. Instead, in our view we have juxtaposed a human figure, which illustrates even more strikingly the contrast in scale. This colossal statue was installed in the apsidal end of the great hall of the vaulted Basilica of Maxentius or Constantine in the Roman Forum. Its purpose was to symbolize the presence of the great ruler, who might have in fact been present in person to address the crowds, but not visible to them, much as today's jumbotron screens aggrandize political figures at conventions and rallies, since their actual forms would be dwarfed by the colossal spaces.

Examples of colossal scale abound at the Basilica of Saint Peter. Visitors are amazed when they are told that the entirety of the elevation of the Palazzo Farnese can easily be accommodated within the space under the dome, and is approximately the same height as the Bernini's baldacchino. The heads of the infant putti who flank and cavort around the holy water basins at the bases of the nave piers are, like the statue of Constantine, many times human scale.[6] In both of these examples, such large-scale elements are used to impress.

---

6   Blanchard, Jeffrey. In on site lectures in Saint Peter's.

17. Colossal head of Constantine, Court, Capitoline Museum [P. 67, Illustration 126]

18. Michelangelo, Rear Façade, St. Peter's. [P. 67, Illustration 128]

Chapter 9.
The Inside and the Outside

The theme of this chapter is the enclosure of interior space and the nature of the boundary between exterior and interior, as well as the strategy of layering zones of increasingly defined, private interior space.

> **19. Maritime Theater, Hadrian's Villa, Tivoli [Page 70, Illustration 138]**
>
> A building can include things within things as well as spaces within spaces. And its interior configurations can contrast with its container in other ways besides those of the Villa Savoye's. The circular perimeters of bearing wall and colonnade in Hadrian's Maritime Theater at Tivoli produce another version of the same spatial idea.

Hadrian's Villa, located less than an hour's travel from the center of Rome in the plain below the picturesque hamlet of Tivoli, is well worth the trip, and can be combined with the Villa d'Este, a splendid water garden designed by Pirro Ligorio. The ancient villa, the magnum opus and country retreat of the Roman emperor Hadrian, was built between 118 and 134 CE. Following its abandonment, it was forgotten and only rediscovered in the Renaissance. The ruined architectural forms provided great architectural inspiration to Borromini and artistic inspiration to Piranesi. Its irregular and complex plan was influenced by the sloping topography of the site, and the desire to accommodate the flow of water across it. We can imagine the sun-baked plazas and surfaces we discover today, cool and animated with the movement and sound of flowing water.

The maritime theater, or island enclosure is still blessed with water, and the solid circular enclosing wall contrasts with the lighter and more fanciful successive rings of inner boundary. First there is an ionic colonnade concentric with the outer solid wall, separating the walkway from the circular moat. A circular island then has a series of alternating solid and transparent openings leading to a central inner sanctum whose shape is defined by four convex curved lintels resting on four columns. It is a unique place, thought to be the inner sanctum and private retreat of Hadrian. Charles Moore, Venturi's contemporary and Princeton colleague in the 1950s, was fascinated by this place and describes it as follows:

> At the east end of this great wall, past the Hall of the Philosophers, is the circular area that makes a pivot point on the plan and is, more than any other single place, the focus and the heart of the villa. It is called the Maritime Theater, or the Natatorium, but neither of these names makes any sense. It is a round island, surrounded by a moat, which is surrounded with a colonnade, which in turn is backed by a circular wall. The

island was reached only by two retractable bridges in Hadrian's time. As we have seen, in the villa water was used everywhere, creating with its flow an image of distance, furthermore creating an image of immersion. But here in this round place the water is made to create the image of an island, with all the sense of withdrawal and independence that an island implies. Here in this vast jungle of ruins is an inviolate place, a perfect circle surrounded by water, with a stronger sense of place than anywhere else in the villa.

On the island are incredibly small rooms, and in the center of it all is a tiny atrium, square with concave sides, which must have had a fountain, a source of active moving water, which would have lost itself in the still water of the moat around. What went on in the rooms is anybody's guess, but it was surely something very special.

In this essay, published in 1960 in *Perspecta, the Yale Architecture Journal*, it is clear that Charles Moore was also looking at familiar sites with new eyes, albeit with an eye less focused on the highly formal questions that Venturi was grappling with and more on issues of habitation and place.

20. Santa Maria Maggiore [P. 71, Illustration 142]

Fuga's walls wrap around S. Maria Maggiore, and Soane's walls enclose the distorted intricacies of courtyards and wings of the Bank of England in the same way and for similar reasons: they unify outside in relation to the scale of the city, the contradictory spatial intricacies of chapels or banking rooms which evolve in time. Crowded intricacies can be excluded as well as contained.

21. Bernini Piazza, St. Peter's [P. 72, Illustration 144]

The colonnades at St. Peter's and at the Piazza del Plebiscito in Naples, respectively exclude the intricacies of the Vatican Palace complex and the city complex, in order to achieve unity for their piazzas.

Fuga's walls and Bernini's colonnade are about 90 years apart, and are part of two of the most important and holy sites in Rome. They both aim to present an image of order and ceremonial grandeur in building complexes that evolved over time, beginning with their early Christian origins as basilicas in the fourth and fifth centuries respectively. At the basilica of St. Peter, traces of the original five-aisled fourth century basilica are gone, although the burial ground beneath it for early Christians can be visited. Images of the original basilica, partially demolished to make way for Bramante's new central domed structure have also been preserved, and to get an idea of how the piazza looked before Bernini's colonnade was installed, one may view a painting depicting the scene. It is hung in the excellent Museo di Roma in the Palazzo Bracci, adjacent to Piazza Navona. Even with the colonnade in place, the jumble of accretions to the Vatican palace are in clear view above Bernini's colonnade on the north, the right side as you face the basilica.

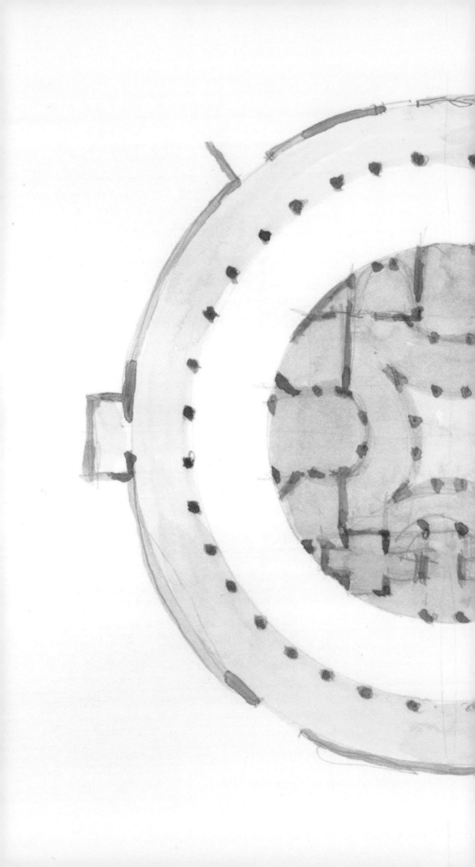

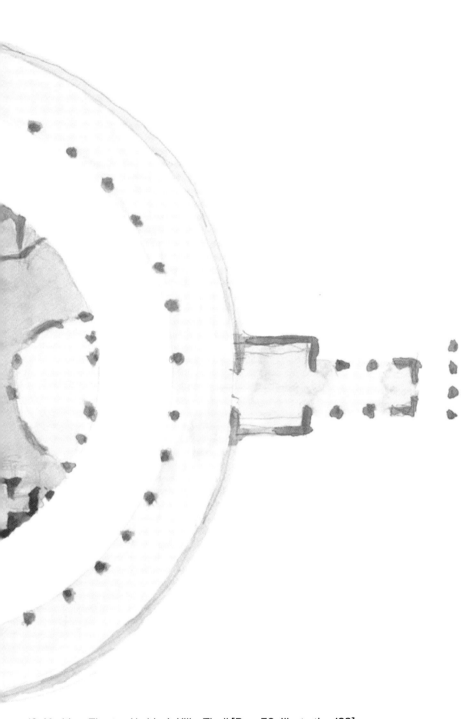

19. Maritime Theater, Hadrian's Villa, Tivoli [Page 70, Illustration 138]

20. Santa Maria Maggiore [P. 71, Illustration 142]

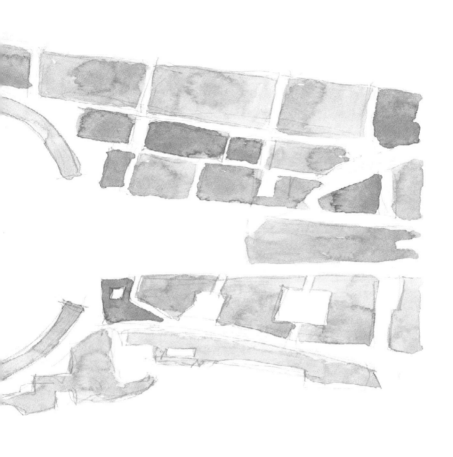

21. Bernini Piazza, St. Peter's [P. 72, Illustration 144]

The palimpsest of layered additions and changes to Santa Maria Maggiore is easier to detect. The original three-aisled basilica remains and can be clearly identified in the aerial view which was used as Venturi's illustration, and which we have captured in watercolor. Inside, the nave is lined by the original colonnades of reused Roman columns brought from other structures, but the ceiling and the arches that interrupt the nave at the transepts are later additions. The bell tower was added in the 14th century. Michelangelo's Sforza Chapel, one of his last works, was added between 1560 and 1573. Next, the two large domed chapels prominent in our image, the Sistine (right) and the Pauline (left) Chapels were added a quarter century later in 1585-90 and 1605-15, and were designed by Domenico Fontana and Flaminio Ponzio respectively. They are funerary chapels for Pope Sixtus V, Peretti and Pope Paul V, Borghese. The former, whose reign was short (1585-1590) had a disproportionately large impact on the layout of Rome's urban street pattern as described earlier; much in the way these two architectural enclosures sought to create order from the chaos they contained. Sixtus placed a small obelisk at the apse of Santa Maria Maggiore, visible in the aerial view, to terminate his street beginning at the top of the Spanish steps. The symmetrical design of the apse and grand steps designed by Carlo Rainaldi in 1673 give the basilica the importance it deserves.

22. Castel Sant'Angelo [P. 72, Illustration 146]

Sometimes the contradiction is not between the inside and the outside but between the top and the bottom of the building...In the Castel Sant' Angelo the rectangular elements evolve from a circular base.

The Castel Sant'Angelo was transformed from what had been Hadrian's Tomb. To get an idea of how it would have appeared, one need only travel the short distance to the Mausoleum of Augustus, whose original circular form is preserved. Interestingly, in this case the process of transition is the reverse of the previous examples. A pure original form becomes more complex over time with additions, which in this case are structures added to the top of the solid cylindrical tomb for accommodation of the popes taking refuge in the fortified castle. The original structure has a system of original circular and radial passageways added in the medieval period for access, and there is a rectangular core that contains a series of four cubic rooms, one on top of another, and this element is visible as the central crenellated tower. One of the great fascinations of a visit here is to try to figure out where one is within the structure at any given time. There are also magnificent Renaissance interiors and from the top, great views of the surrounding city.

22. Castel Sant'Angelo [P. 72, Illustration 146]
Perspective sketch exterior

22. Castel Sant'Angelo [P. 72, Illustration 146]
Diagram

23. Cortona, Santa Maria della Pace [P. 73. Illustration 150]

In S. Maria Della Pace the super-imposition of enclosing elements, which are successively convex, perpendicular, and then concave, became contrasting things behind things to work transitions between the outside and the inside.

This is one of Rome's most intimate, intricate, and at the same time, dramatic urban stage sets. The design by Pietro da Cortona, was commissioned by Pope Alexander VII. An existing church and monastery was to be expanded with an enlarged forecourt to accommodate the carriages of the noble parishioners. Parts of buildings on either side were demolished, and a unified façade treatment was created for the entire square. The convex projecting porch and gently swelling façade above, capped by two superimposed pediments, seem to be freestanding in front of a concave backdrop which incorporates narrow lanes on either side. The prospect is constantly evolving as one approaches along the angled streets leading to it. Initially the prospect is a flat tableau which takes on increasing three-dimensionality as one approaches, and finally is immersed in the composition. The church (open only Monday, Wednesday, Saturday, and Sunday mornings and occasionally for a 6pm mass) contains Raphael frescos, and through a separate entrance to the left of the church porch, one discovers the magnificent cloister by Bramante, his first work in Rome dating from 1500 to 1504.

24. Rosati (main architect for church) and Soria (architect of façade, S. Carlo ai Catinari, Rome, Chapel of Santa Cecilia, Antonio Gherardi (architect of Chapel of SAnta Cecelia, 1692-1700)[Page 76-77, illus 170]

The multiple domes of the S. Cecilia Chapel in S. Carlo ai Catinari in Rome are detached and contrasting in shape. Beyond the oval oculus of the lower dome is seen a rectangular space flooded with light, containing a sculptural quartet of musical angels. Beyond this zone, in turn, floats an even more brilliant oval lantern.

The general theme in these pages is layering ("unattached linings") and the enclosure of spaces within other spaces, often "contrasting in shape, position, pattern and size" [p 74]. The third chapel on the right of this Baroque, Latin cross church is dedicated to Santa Cecilia. She is the patron of music, and this richly layered composition seems to billow up, as if swelling on the chords of a crescendo. It has been called the "paradise" chapel, and perhaps we can also interpret it as an embodiment of the saint's ascension into that realm after her martyrdom at the hands of a third century Roman soldier when she refused to consummate a forced marriage. During the marriage ceremony, it is said, she sat apart singing to God.

23. Cortona, Santa Maria della Pace [P. 73. Illustration 150]
Ariel view

23. Cortona, Santa Maria della Pace [P. 73. Illustration 150]
Perspective of square

24. Rosati (main architect for church) and Soria (architect of façade, S. Carlo ai Catinari, Rome, Chapel of Santa Cecilia, Antonio Gherardi (architect of Chapel of Santa Cecelia, 1692-1700)[Page 76-77, illus 170]

Light is the medium through which the drama of the architectural forms is conveyed. The lower, earthly realm of the observer is shrouded in obscurity. Light is introduced mysteriously from a hidden source above (actually clerestory windows in a lantern above the dome). As the eye travels upward each surface is bathed in light of increasing intensity as the hidden source is reached. The play of light and shadow is dramatized by the contour of the ornament-laden surfaces including choirs of angels playing instruments. These are on the pendentives supporting the first elliptical dome, on panels on the four axes of that dome, and finally, they appear as dark silhouettes perched on the ring of the dome's opening or oculus. Their dark, backlit forms further dramatize the contrast between the dark lower realms as opposed to the upper regions bathed in light. Finally, it all terminates in a shallow saucer dome with a golden dove in the center.

The space has been represented through a gradual layering of progressively darker watercolor washes that tell the story of the progression into light, along with the sculptural and architectural relief and the shadows they cast.

25. Brasini, Church of the Cuore Immaculata di Maria Santissima, Rome (1923-36) [Page 77, illus 172-173]

Armando Brasini's neo-Baroque church of the Cuore Immaculata di Maria Santissima (1923-51) in (Parioli) Rome has a quasi-circular plan containing a Greek Cross plan. The Greek cross plan is reflected on the outside in four pedimented porches marking the ends of the cross. These porches in turn are made convex to accommodate to the circular plan.

Built during the fascist era, this church embodies the polemical position held by the Roman Catholic Church and the Mussolini regime, both of which turned to a language of traditional neo-baroque architecture for symbolic purposes. What is seen today is but one-third of the intended composition, the base on which a soaring dome was to rise to three times the height of the story we see today.

The point Venturi makes about the plan geometry of cross and circle superimposed, recalls his discussion of San Carlo alle Quattro Fontane (7). The play of light across the deep recesses created by voids, flanked by columns in antis, dramatizes the way the forms appear, carved out of the masonry mass of travertine and brick.

We can imagine that Venturi delighted in the fact that this highly traditional design was promulgated at the same time as Le Corbusier's *Vers Une Architecture Nouvelle* and Johnson and Hitchcock's *The International Style*. Its massive forms stand in stark contrast to the lightness championed in both of those works.

25. Brasini, Church of the Cuore Immaculata di Maria Santissima, Rome (1923-36) [Page 77, illus 172-173]

26. Gregorini and Passalacqua, S. Croce in Gerusalemme
[Page 78, Illustration 176]

In the vestibule of S. Croce in Gerusalemme and in the interiors of SS. Sergius and Bacchus (Istanbul) and of St. Stephen Walbrook (London) it is the series of columns which define the inner, detached and contrasting layer of enclosure. These supports, along with the domes above them, make the intraspatial relationships of the interior.

Although early in its foundation in Constantinian times, the latest of the seven holy basilicas in its current architectural form is located near the Aurelian Walls at the southeastern edge of the city. The design is also about the last exemplar of the baroque style, before architectural expression would give way to the neoclassical. The present structure, built between 1740 and 1758, was preceded by an early Christian basilica in 324, the original papal basilica. Its symbolic importance was grounded in the fact that it housed a relic of the true cross, brought back from Jerusalem, as the name states. The original basilica was built within a palace and this may explain the current design, with the grand baroque entrance facade embedded in a palace façade on either side. It served as a double-functioning element for the entrance to basilica and palace alike. This may explain the practical derivation for the plan with the oval vestibule and ambulatory wrapped around it. The palace doors on either side establish the longitudinal axis of the rotunda, which is perpendicular to the axis of the basilica. The ambulatories offer direct access to these doors by providing a path independent of the oval vestibule. The expression of the four main axes with arched openings and adjacent rectangular openings suggests a Palladian or Serlian arch, and the basilica axis is emphasized by the use of columns *in antis* flanking its wider openings.

27. Michelangelo, Sforza Chapel, S. Maria Maggiore
[P. 79, Illustrations 181-183]

Layers are implied in Michelangelo's Sforza Chapel in S. Maria Maggiore in the violent penetrations of rectangular space and curved space in plan and of barrel vaults, domes and niche-vaulting in section. The ambiguous juxtaposition of these two kinds of shapes as well as the implied intense compression and enormous scale of the flatly curved spaces (which by implication extend beyond the actual enclosure) give this interior its particular power and tension.

This chapel was added to the zone between the side aisle of the early Christian basilica and what would later become the outside perimeter of the later enclosing façade. It is reserved as a place of quiet prayer, and access must be requested of the monks in the sacristy to the right of the basilica's entrance. It was one of Michelangelo's last works, when he was almost 90, begun in 1560 for Cardinal Guido Ascanio Sforza and completed in 1564 after Michelangelo's

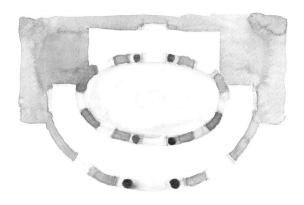

26. Gregorini and Passalacqua, S. Croce in Gerusalemme [Page 78, Illustration 176]

death. The geometry Michelangelo used, and the suggestion Venturi makes that this small space implies an imaginary larger structure beyond its boundaries are ingenious and intriguing. Geometric in plan, the proportions are defined by double squares and these squares become double cubes, the rectangular space Venturi references. The width and the depth are equal, and the nave and "transepts" would define a Greek cross except for the fact that the cross axis is shifted closer to the entrance in order to define a deeper space for the altar. Michelangelo was also interested in central plans at this time, and he was engaged in the design of San Giovanni dei Fiorentini,[7] of which the early plans were centric. A central plan here is suggested by the four columns which step in front of the defining squares and intrude within the space and support a rounded handkerchief vault above. The "flatly curved spaces" on either side of these columnar openings, where the funereal monuments are located, imply a circular building in plan. They are in fact segments of the arc that defines that circle. If a hemispherical dome (like that of the Pantheon) were placed on this drum it would be slightly above the existing square vault, which would then take on the form of a baldachino in the larger space. Of course there is no way to know whether this is what Michelangelo had in mind, but it is a tribute to his genius that the design invites and supports interpretations like these. It should be noted that the natural lighting today is totally different from what was originally intended. There was to be one window over the central altar, giving it a back-lit aspect, and three windows each in the lateral wings—one above in the blind opening and two flanking the tombs. The windows would have further emphasized the lateral spaces and the larger imaginary space implied by large curves.

---

7   See entry on this building in Stefan Grundmann, The Architecture of Rome, Axel Menges, p. 157.

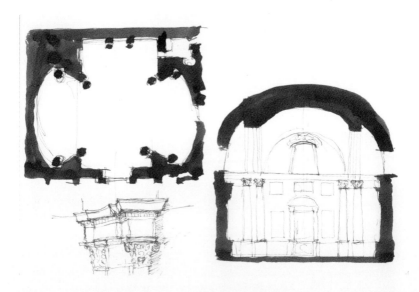

27. Michelangelo, Sforza Chapel, S. Maria Maggiore [P. 79, Illustrations 181-183]

Top left: Watercolor reflected ceiling plan

Bottom left: Watercolor plan and section and pencil sketch

Top right: Watercolor sketch axonometric

Bottom right: Watercolor sketch perspective

28. Vignola. Villa Giulia [P. 80, Illustration 187]

In Charles V's palace at Granada, the Villa Farnese at Caprarola, and the Villa Giulia, the courtyards dominate because they are large and their shapes contrast with the shape of the perimeters. They make the primary space; the rooms of the palaces are leftover space.

The Villa Giulia is one of several important *Ville Suburbane* built by papal or noble patrons on the outskirts of Rome during the Renaissance. This villa was built by Pope Julius III just north of Porta del Popolo, and today it houses the National Museum of Etruscan Art. It was constructed in two phases with the first, the front part, built from 1550-1555 by Vignola, and the second enclosure, the Nympheum from 1555 by Ammanati and Vasari. Indeed, the clarity of the layered space within the courtyard is far stronger than the block of the villa surrounding, which in the case of the Villa Giulia is not a pure geometric shape but a composite of several rectangular wings. The defining shape of the interior courtyard is an extended rectangle with a semicircular end, which is located at the point of entry. A vaulted semicircular portico within the mass of the building defines an interstitial strip of space between the inner enclosing walls and an outer garden zone. Halfway along the rectangular court is a raised pavilion whose dimensions in plan compare to the first entry foyer, and it introduces a second semicircular enclosure, in this case a sunken court reached by a curving flight steps along the walls on either side. In the

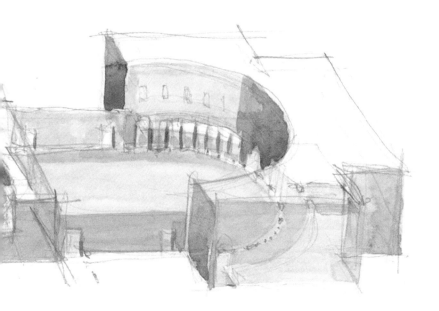

28. Vignola. Villa Giulia [P. 80, Illustration 187]

center of the space is a smaller sunken court, the nympheum, one level down with a shape in proportion to the semicircle extended by the straight sides used by the two previous spaces. These successive enclosures in plan are like Russian dolls one inside the other.

The spaces, complexly layered in plan and in section created an exotic threshold for the pope and his guests between the city and the country. The villa would have been the scene of exotic gatherings featuring alfresco dining, befitting an ancient Roman villa. Julius was a great collector of Roman objects, and there would have been many such objects to embellish the villa and its gardens, including a large circular fountain of monolithic porphyry. One can see it now in the round hall of Hercules in the Pio Clementine wing of the Vatican museums.

In 1950, Franco Minissi was commissioned to design a series of gallery installations for the display of what is certainly one of the best and most extensive collections of Etruscan art. His modernist but eclectic design provides a lively mixture of new and old materials and an entirely new layer and identity in the interior of the building. The showcases are elegant artifacts in their own right and function as "guests" or variable contingent pre-existing structures in the museum spaces. This is one of Italy's best museum rehabilitations of the 1950s when Carlo Scarpa and Franco Albini were doing signature works. It is also the only one of the great installation designs of this era that is in Rome. Minissi's installation uses elegant and delicate glass and bronze vitrines to float the Etruscan material within the Renaissance villa with a formal vocabulary distinct from both. Taking the notion of the vitrine to its extreme, Minissi floats clouds of Etruscan pottery in planes of glass held together with the most minimal custom machined dowels, clips and brackets. This collage of ancient art, Renaissance architecture and Modernist exhibition furniture could be seen as a precursor to Venturi's understanding of simultaneous contrast. Recent updates to the installation have improved accessibility to the collection and objects, however, they have changed aspects of Minissi's design.

29. Piazza San Ignazio [P. 85, Illustration 201]
Grey Walls is a rural Piazza S. Ignazio.

In a section dealing with circular and curved enclosures of space, this brief reference compares Rome's most stage-like piazza with the English country house Greywalls, designed by Edwin Lutyens in 1901. The main point concerns "outside-dominant" space, or what was termed in our architecture school a "dominant void." Piazza San Ignazio, designed by Filippo Raguzzini in 1727 is certainly all about the creation of clearly definable open urban spaces. The buildings – of which there are as many as five separate ones, some joined at the rear to previously existing buildings – are not palaces or important institutional buildings. They are in fact speculative buildings for apartments. Somewhat in the same way segments of curves define larger implied shapes as in the Sforza Chapel, the facades suggest shapes that are completed in the imagination, and this can best be perceived by looking up at the cornice, where the building meets the sky, as shown in one of our illustrations. In this way a large ellipse is flanked by two smaller ones. The large figure is centered on the axis of the earlier 17th century Church of Sant Ignazio, and the smaller elliptical spaces align with the row of circular side chapels flanking the nave. It is most surprising to come upon this space by accident, emerging from the chaotic tangle of one of the many streets leading into it, and discover emerging order by looking up at the cornices and observing the consistent detail from one building to another. One has entered an orderly designed realm, built as a homage to the complications in intersections of the rapidly changing urban life of early eighteenth century Rome.

29. Piazza San Ignazio [P. 85, Illustration 201]
Bottom image: Perspective of facades combined with plan

Perspective view

Just steps from the American Academy on the Gianicolo Hill, the entire cascade of terraces, stairs, walls, and a grotto is a virtual minuet of movement through space. On a small private scale, it resembles the movement through space of the Spanish steps, and it was long thought that its architect, Francesco De Sanctis designed the Arcadian Academy. This is not certain, and another designer considered possible was Antonio Canevari. The dates of its creation are 1693 to 1731. Access may be arranged by contacting the Accademia degli Arcadi with a request. This space, also known as the Bosco Parrasio belongs to an exclusive eighteenth century literary society, and it was created as a place for its members, dressed in Greek togas, to gather and read classic texts, and to enact the tragedies. One of the group's objectives was the eradication of "bad taste" as exemplified by the Baroque. The elliptical amphitheater, framed by the curved façade Venturi describes, is the space created for those gatherings. The garden was meant to represent a pastoral retreat, a place of simplicity and beauty removed from the horrors of the Baroque city below.

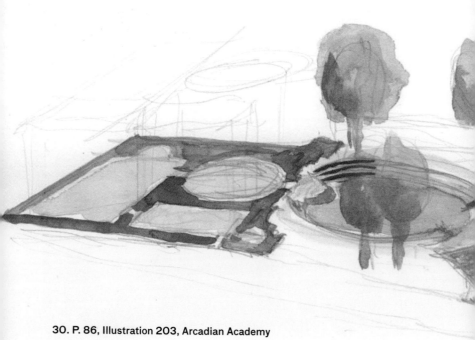

30. P. 86, Illustration 203, Arcadian Academy
Axonometric plan

30. P. 86, Illustration 203, Arcadian Academy
Sketch view

Chapter 10.
The Obligation Toward the Difficult Whole

The focus of this chapter is composition of building elevations and masses, and how a building comprised of a collection of parts can come together to make – with difficulty – a complete composition. The very idea of considering the compositional effect of a building would have been anathema to the architectural modernist of the mid-twentieth century, and this fact, not to mention some of the examples cited below, makes the concluding chapter of the book perhaps the most revolutionary of all.

> **31. Brasini, Orphanage of Il Buon Pastore**
> **[P. 92, Illustrations 218, 219, and 220]**
> The varying configurations of the wings and windows, roofs and ornaments of the orphanage of the Buon Pastore (1929-34) near Rome are an orgy of inflections of enormous scope similar to the scale of Blenheim. This neo-Baroque complex by Armando Brazini, (bizarre in 1940 and admittedly questionable for an asylum for little girls) astonishingly composes a multitude of diverse parts into a difficult whole. At all levels of scale it is an example of inflections within inflections successively directed toward different centers—toward the short façade in the front, or the anticlimactically small dome near the center of the complex, with its unusually big cupola. When you stand close enough to see a smaller element of inflection you sometimes need to turn almost 180 degrees to see its counterpart at a great distance. An element of suspense is introduced when you move around the enormous building. You are aware of elements related by inflection to elements already seen or not yet seen, like the unraveling of a symphony. As a fragment in plan and elevation, the asymmetrical composition of each wing is wrought with tensions and implications concerning the symmetrical whole.

Venturi, with narrative straight face, analyzes what most architects of his time, and many even now, would consider the kitsch 20th century Baroque pastiche work of Brasini as if it were by Bernini. One of the most important overall achievements of *Complexity and Contradiction* may be the way Venturi accepts the evidence he discovered around him in Rome, without prejudice or value judgment based on its lineage or lack thereof. In fact it was his writing that opened the eyes of many of his sympathetic contemporaries, not only to Brasini, but a whole stable of early twentieth century architects (Lutyens, Plecnic, etc.) who had somehow "missed the boat" and failed to respond to the siren call of Modernism. It was a thrilling revelation to Venturi and his contemporaries to discover that an alternative architecture of tradition persisted in the mid-twentieth century.

32. Piazza del Popolo [P. 92, Illustration 221]

At the scale of the town, inflection can come from the position of elements which are in themselves uninflected. In the Piazza del Popolo the domes of the twin churches confirm each building as a separate whole, but their single towers, symmetrical themselves, become inflective because of their asymmetrical positions on each church. In the context of the piazza each building is a fragment of a greater whole and a part of a gateway to the Corso.

The Piazza del Popolo has always been the "front door" of Rome. It stands within the Aurelian walls and has served as the first point of entry to the city for travelers arriving from the north, which is to say, the rest of Europe, even from Roman times. A Roman road, called, the via Lata, ran straight through and on to the Capitoline hill in the center of the ancient city. The site became a true piazza and received is designation in the 15th century when the church of Santa Maria del Popolo was re-constructed within the city gate. From that time onward, the form of the square gradually evolved by stages to the elegant form we appreciate today, largely the design of Giuseppe Valadier completed in 1824, but only perfected with the elimination of vehicular traffic in the late 1990s. As earlier described, Pope Sixtus V placed an obelisk in the center of the square as a nodal point anchoring the three axial streets that form the "Trident." Via Ripetta, via del Corso, and via del Babuino would form part of his imagined axial movement system through Rome.[8] Approximately 100 years after Sixtus V, one of the next great builder-Popes, Alexander VII wanted to create a fitting pair of landmarks to frame the Trident. A ceremonial gate, designed by Bernini, had already been erected to commemorate the arrival of Queen Cristina of Sweden in 1655 (carried on a couch designed by Bernini, no less). A Protestant, she had converted to Catholicism, and so became a strong symbol of the appeal of the faith. There was only one religious order that required a church on the square, but Alexander, seizing the opportunity for symmetry, called for another one to be built, resulting in the pair we see today. The churches are not strictly symmetrical, if one studies them closely. The domes are quite different, and the church on the left, Santa Maria in Montesanto (1662-75) is oval in plan and has a narrower width, while Santa Maria dei Miracoli, (1675 – 79) is circular and presents a wider dome. These details do not impair the appearance of symmetry, and the linking of the two in a gateway was reinforced later in the 18th century by the addition of asymmetrical towers flanking the central axis of via del Corso.

---

8   Edmund Bacon coined this term in his presentation of the urban planning of Sixtus V in Design of Cities, published in 1967.

31. Brasini, Orphanage of Il Buon Pastore [P. 92, Illustrations 218, 219, and 220]

32. Piazza del Popolo [P. 92, Illustration 221]

Conclusion

Fifty years have passed since the publication of *Complexity and Contradiction in Architecture*. We have retraced Venturi's steps through Rome, discovering a much longer continuum, and along the way added our own observations rooted in our own experiences through those years. What light has been shed in the half-century's passage of time and change in architectural discourse, much of which was unleashed by Venturi's text itself? How has the role of Rome in forming the sensibilities of a young architect changed during this time? The period from 1966 to 2016 has witnessed great changes in architectural practice, of which the revolutionary tremors Venturi introduced were only the beginning. The publication of *Complexity and Contradiction* came when society as a whole was poised for the radical changes of the late sixties and early seventies, when protests against the war in Vietnam coalesced into a wholesale questioning of the foundations of society and government, as it was then known. It would be tempting to conclude that Venturi's wholesale jettisoning of the strictures of architectural practice was a manifestation of this broader societal trend, but the fact that the gestation of Venturi's work preceded these manifestations, and also the nature of it is so focused on a deeply analytical approach that is rooted in the aesthetics and appearance of architecture and not its social or political implications, suggests that fomenting revolution in its broad sense could not have been further from his intention.

In this sense, the coincidence of Venturi's work and cataclysmic societal upheaval may follow the phenomenon described by George Kubler in his seminal theoretical work, *The Shape of Time*. In that short, but dense and rich book describing "the history of things," Kubler lays out a theory for why stylistic and artistic trends develop the way they do. The role of the individual genius creator is tied to an overall schema for the unfolding of the evolution of artistic expression. What determines the elevation of the work of one practitioner over another is thus the degree to which the individual work fits with the broader currents that are evolving. In this way, it can be said that Venturi's highly focused and personal approach came at just the right moment when the winds of change were ready to fill his sails and carry him forward.

And of course we now know how significant the changes in architectural thought were. Many of us remember the opening of an exhibition at the Museum of Modern Art devoted to the architecture of the Ecole de Beaux Arts in 1975. At the opening symposium, the Curator of Architecture, Arthur Drexler, pronounced in that hallowed shrine of the modern movement in art and architecture, "modern architecture is dead." The literal use of historical elements in architectural expression which dominated the following decade or so was termed Postmodernism, but it is important to note that neither

Venturi nor Charles Moore considered themselves postmodern architects, but rather considered themselves part of the continuing tradition of modernism in which they were formed. Many consider the failure of the historical expression of postmodernism to be a result of a lack of rigor in the manner in which historical forms were adapted and executed using methods and materials that were neither authentic in means of composition or design nor in materials of execution, since the commercial buildings that were being built were largely constructed of modern materials of steel, glass, concrete and plaster and not dressed stone. Those who remained dedicated to the tenets of modern architecture, as well as a small contingent of practitioners who favored authentic traditional design using canonical principles of classical composition and construction with traditional materials both condemned the free wheeling use of historical forms that was postmodernism, and the movement lost its steam by the 1990s.

Changes to architectural expression and practice—far more sweeping than anything that was experienced in the latter decades of the twentieth century— are underway now. These are the result of the "perfect storm" convergence of new ways of visualization, representation, and fabrication as represented by computer and imaging technology, and the rise of multiple "ethical" concerns applied to the creation of buildings, cities and places. These highlight a concern for the environment by wisely using the finite resources we have, including sources of energy, materials, and the public purse. In addition, today's architect does not just answer to an emperor or pope, as was the case for most of the buildings we have examined together in Rome, but each design process must successfully navigate a complex process of participation and review involving the true diversity of today's society, which is celebrated for its degree of inclusion. Today's architectural designer seemingly finds little time to engage in the kind of speculation about the refinement of proportion of a window, façade, or plan detail, which may seem trivial in the context of addressing global warming, or the rampant growth of cities increasingly filled with the underserved and underrepresented, and whose continuing existence on the planet is challenged by the changes to the climate we have caused.

The Rome we have examined with Venturi might seem to have little to say about these challenges and the changes in architecture of the last half century. Unlike other cities in Europe (London and Berlin, to name two), it was mercifully spared the ravages of war, and the subsequent ravages of modernist urban design, now often being reversed in those cities. While there were significant post 1870 changes within the Aurelian walls with the urbanization of the "desabitato" or vacant aresa, there were some significant buildings built in Rome in this period, including the work of Nervi and his partners for the Olympics of 1960, two buildings by Richard Meier and one by Zaha Hadid, with the exception of Meier's Ara Pacis Museum, none were built within the historic center inside the Aurelian walls, and so that urban fabric remains much as it was represented in Gianbattista Nolli's great plan of 1748.

Does this mean that Rome no longer holds the lessons it did for Venturi and all those who preceded him at the American Academy and those of other nations, all founded to give their constituents a chance to learn firsthand from the source? Many would say that the sort of concerns and types of study traditionally engaged in are now quaint and not relevant to today's challenges. But we believe that the lessons that the history and form of the architecture and urbanism of Rome – as it has evolved over two millennia, and a tiny fraction of which we have explored in these pages – is ever more critical to us today. The story the stones and waters of Rome tell us is about how we as individuals and societies create meaning and focus in our confusing times. We endow the places we choose to inhabit and the edifices we erect to house our prized institutions with great care in order to ennoble our existence on this earth. There is nowhere else, where we can trace in urban and architectural form the manifestations of the cataclysmic shifts in population and influence that Rome experienced. For example, the city's population declined from an all time high of a million inhabitants at the height of the Roman empire in the second century CE to less than 20,000 less than a millennium later. There may be other places that can boast similar change, but they do not have the layers of physical evidence that Rome has, and cannot tell us their stories. These are the reasons why Venturi and so many others have devoted lifetimes to a study of Rome's secrets, and we hope our readers will make *la Citta Èterna* forever theirs.

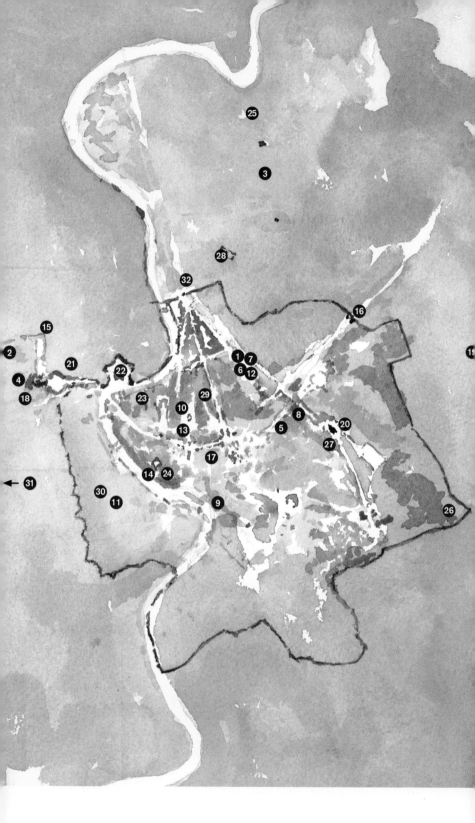

Left: Sketch map of Rome with locations of the sites identified by Robert Venturi and the subject of this book. For actual way finding, the addresses on page 109-112 will work with gps or with the excellent map produced by the Touring Club Italiano.

1. Palazzo di Propaganda Fide, Bernini Façade (1644)
2. Casino di Pio IV, Vatican (1562)
3. Casa Girasole, (1947-50)
4. Rear Façade, St. Peter's, (1546-93)
5. Sant' Andrea al Quirinale, (1658-70)
6. Palazzo di Propaganda Fide, Chapel of the Re Magi, (1646-66)
7. Palazzo di Propaganda Fide, Rome, Interior room (1646-66)
8. San Carlo alle Quattro Fontane, (1638-41)
9. S. Maria in Cosmedin, (c. 780, 1120-23)
10. Pantheon, (118-125)
11. S. Maria dei Sette Dolori (1642-1665)
12. Palazzo di Propaganda Fide, Side façade by Borromini (1646-1666)
13. Palazzo Massimo, (1532-38)
14. Palazzo Farnese Rear Façade, (1516-1534)
15. Belvedere Court, Vatican, (1503-1523)
16. Porta Pia, (1561-1564)
17. Capitoline Museum, Court containing Colossal head of Constantine, (c. 312)
18. Rear Façade, St. Peter's, (1546-1593)
19. Hadrian's Villa, Maritime Theater, Tivoli, (118-134)
20. Santa Maria Maggiore, (432-440, 1585-1590, 1740)
21. Piazza, St. Peter's, Bernini Colonnade, (1657-1667)
22. Castel Sant'Angelo, (135-139, 1514-1516)
23. Santa Maria della Pace, (1482, 1500-1504, 1656-1667)
24. San Carlo ai Catinari, Chapel of Santa Cecilia, (1612-1650, 1691-1700)
25. Church of the Cuore Immaculata di Maria Santissima, (1923-36)
26. S. Croce in Gerusalemme, (1741-1744)
27. S. Maria Maggiore, Sforza Chapel, (1560-1573)
28. Villa Giulia, (1550-1565)
29. Piazza San Ignazio, (1727-28)
30. Arcadian Academy, (1724)
31. Orphanage of Il Buon Pastore, (1929-1943)
32. Piazza del Popolo, (1661-1679, 1793-1824)

Appendix

Site location, contact, and access information

Chapter 3

1. Gianlorenzo Bernini, Façade, Palazzo di Propaganda Fide, Rome, (1644)
Piazza di Spagna and Via di Propaganda, 1, 00187 Roma
39 06 6988 0162
http://www.museopropagandafide.va/
Visible from public way.

2. Ligorio, Casina di Pio IV, Vatican, Rome (1562)
Vatican Gardens, 00120 Vatican City, Roma
+39 06 6988 3451
http://www.casinapioiv.va/content/accademia/en/about/casina.html
The Casina Pio IV is a patrician villa in Vatican City which is now home to the Pontifical Academy of Sciences, the Pontifical Academy of Social Sciences and the Pontifical Academy of St. Thomas Aquinas. It is only accessible by prior arrangement, and at this writing visits have been suspended.

3. Luigi Moretti, Apartment Building (Casa Girasole), Rome (1947-50)
viale Bruno Bozzi, 64, 00197 Roma
Visible from public way.

Chapter 4

4. Michelangelo, Rear Façade, St. Peter's, Rome (1546-93)
Vatican Gardens, 00120 Vatican City, Roma
06 69883145.
http://www.museivaticani.va/content/museivaticani/en/visita-i-musei/scegli-la-visita/ville-pontificie-e-giardini/giardini-vaticani/giardini-vaticani.html.
Visible from Vatican Gardens, for which permission is required, or enrollment in a guided tour.

5. Bernini, Sant' Andrea al Quirinale, Rome (1658-70).
Via del Quirinale, 30, 00187 Roma
+39 06 487 4565.
http://santandrea.gesuiti.it/.
Active church, accessible during normal opening hours as indicated on website.

6. Borromini, Church of the Re Magi, Palazzo di Propaganda Fide, Rome (1646-66) .
Via di Propaganda, 1, 00187 Roma
+39 06 6988 0162.
http://www.museopropagandafide.va/.
Currently the museum within this building is closed indefinitely. The chapel and other interior spaces may be accessible upon request.

7. Interior room, Borromini, Palazzo di Propaganda Fide, Rome (1646-66) .
Via di Propaganda, 1, 00187 Roma
+39 06 6988 0162.
http://www.museopropagandafide.va/.
Currently the museum within this building is closed indefinitely. The chapel and other interior spaces may be accessible upon request.

8. Borromini, San Carlo alle Quattro Fontane, Rome (1638-41).
Via del Quirinale, 23, 00187 Roma
+ 39 06 488 3261.
http://www.sancarlino.eu/index1.asp
Active church, accessible during normal opening hours as indicated on website.

Chapter 5

9. S. Maria in Cosmedin, Rome, (c. 780, 1120-23).
Piazza della Bocca della Verità, 18, 00186 Roma
+39 06 6787759.
http://060608.it/en/cultura-e-svago/luoghi-di-culto-di-interesse-storico-artistico/chiese-cattoliche/basilica-di-santa-maria-in-cosmedin.html
Active church, accessible during normal opening hours as indicated on website.

10. Pantheon (118-125)
Piazza della Rotonda, 00186 Roma
+39 06 68300230
http://www.polomusealelazio.beniculturali.it/index.php?it/232/pantheon
Active church, accessible during normal opening hours as indicated on website.

11. Borromini, S. Maria dei Sette Dolori (1642-1665).
Via Garibaldi 27, 00153 Roma
http://romanchurches.wikia.com/wiki/Santa_Maria_dei_Sette_Dolori
Chapel, part of what is now a hotel, accessible during business hours.

12. Borromini, Façade, Palazzo di Propaganda Fide (1646-66)
Via di Propaganda, 1, 00187 Roma
Visible from public way.

Chapter 7

13. Peruzzi, Palazzo Massimo alle Colonne (1532-38)
Corso Vittorio Emanuele II, 141,
00186, Roma, Lazio, Italy (Near Piazza Navona and Campo de' Fiori)
+39 06 6878105.
http://www.sgira.org/hm/peruz3.htm
Façade visible from a public way, courtyard requires permission of the on-site portiere to enter.

Chapter 8

14. Michelangelo [in fact Jacopo Barozzi da Vignola, and Giacomo della Porta], Rear Façade, Palazzo Farnese (1516-34).
Piazza Farnese, 67, 00100 Roma (Feature being described is visible from via Giulia on the opposite side).
+39 06 686011.
Online reservation: *www.inventerrome.com*
Palace's rear façade visible from a public way. In order to visit the interior, apply for a tour.

15. Bramante, Belvedere Court, Vatican (1503-23)
00120 Città del Vaticano, Vatican City, Roma
http://vatican.com/articles/info/cortile_del_belvedere-a4147
This façade, bounding the Belvedere Court is accessible by visiting the Vatican Museums.

16. Michelangelo, Porta Pia (1561-64)
Piazzale di Porta Pia, 00179 Roma
The gate faces a public street, accessible at all times.

17. Colossal head of Constantine, Court, Capitoline Museum. (c. 312)
Piazza del Campidoglio, 1, 00186 Roma
+39 06 0608.

http://www.museicapitolini.org/
Entry to the Capitoline Museums is necessary to view this statue in the main courtyard.

18. Michelangelo, Rear Façade, St. Peter's (1546-93)
Piazza San Pietro, 00120 Città del Vaticano, Vatican City.
+39 06 698 83731.
http://www.vatican.va/various/basiliche/san_pietro/index_it.htm
Visible from Vatican Gardens, for which permission is required, or enrollment in a guided tour.

Chapter 9

19. Maritime Theater, Hadrian's Villa, Tivoli (118-134)
Largo Marguerite Yourcenar, 1, 00010 Tivoli RM.
+39 0774 530203.
http://www.coopculture.it/heritage.cfm?id=75#
Hadrian's Villa is an archaeological site open to the public. Tivoli is located approximately 30 km to the east of Rome and can be reached with some effort by metro and bus or by private car.

20. Santa Maria Maggiore (432-440, 1585-1590, 1740)
Piazza di S. Maria Maggiore, 42, 00100 Roma
+39 06 6988 6800
http://www.vatican.va/various/basiliche/sm_maggiore/index_en.html
The exterior (covered in this entry) is accessible from a public way. The interior is an active church open during normal hours.

21. Bernini Piazza, St. Peter's (1657-67)
Piazza San Pietro, 00120 Città del Vaticano, Vatican City.
+39 06 0608.
http://www.vatican.va/various/basiliche/san_pietro/index_it.htm
The square is a public space open at most times.

22. Castel Sant'Angelo (135-139, 1514-1516)
Lungotevere Castello, 50, 00193 Roma
+39 06 6819111.
http://www.castelsantangelo.com/
This is a museum, open during scheduled hours.

23. Cortona, Santa Maria della Pace (1482, 1500-1504, 1656-1667)
Via Arco della Pace 5, Roma, Latium, 00186
+39 06 686 1156.
http://www.chiostrodelbramante.it
or
http://www.060608.it/it/cultura-e-svago/luoghi-di-culto-di-interesse-storico-artistico/chiese-cattoliche/chiesa-santa-maria-della-pace.html
The square and façade are visible at all times, the church is open on a more limited schedule, and the courtyard during the opening hours of the museum.

24. Rosati (main architect for church) and Soria (architect of façade, S. Carlo ai Catinari, Rome, Chapel of Santa Cecilia, Antonio Gherardi (architect of Chapel of Santa Cecelia, 1692-1700).
Piazza Benedetto Cairoli, 117, 00186 Roma
+39 06 6830 7070   or +39 06 6880 9901
http://www.beniculturali.it/mibac/export/MiBAC/index.html#&panel1-1
Active church, accessible during normal opening hours as indicated on website.

25. Brasini, Church of the Cuore Immaculata di Maria Santissima, Rome (1923-36).
Piazza Euclide, 00197 Roma
+39 06 807 4509.
http://www.cuoreimmacolatobari.org/

26. Gregorini and Passalacqua, S. Croce in Gerusalemme (1741-44)
Piazza di S. Croce in Gerusalemme, 00185 Roma
+39 06 7061 3053.
http://www.santacroceroma.it/en/
Active church, accessible during normal opening hours as indicated on website.

27. Michelangelo, Sforza Chapel, S. Maria Maggiore (1560-73)
42 Piazza di Santa Maria Maggiore
00185 Roma
06 44 65 836 / 06 48 14 287
http://www.vatican.va/various/basiliche/sm_maggiore/en/cappella_musicale/cenni_storici.htm
This chapel is reserved for prayer, however in late afternoons after 4 pm, it can be opened on request to the monks in the sacristy to the right of the main entrance of the basilica, or by requesting in advance. The chapel can also be seen through a grille from the nave of the basilica.

28. Vignola. Villa Giulia. Museo Nazionale Etrusco di Villa Giulia (1550-65)
piazzale di Villa Giulia, 900196 Roma
+39 06 3226571.
http://www.villagiulia.beniculturali.it/
This is a museum, open during scheduled hours.

29. Piazza San Ignazio (1727-28)
Via del Caravita, 8A Roma
http://santignazio.gesuiti.it/en/
The square is a public space open at all times.

30. Accademia degli Arcadi (1724).
Piazza Sant'Agostino 8 - 00186 Roma
+39 06.68.40.801 .
http://www.accademiadellarcadia.it/
Private house and garden, access can sometimes be granted on request.

Chapter 10

31. Brasini, Orphanage of Il Buon Pastore (1929-43)
via Silvestri, 301 e via di Bravetta 383, Roma
Parts of this complex are accessible during business hours.

32. Piazza del Popolo (1661-1679, 1793-1824)
Piazza del Popolo, 48121 Roma
http://www.reidsitaly.com/destinations/lazio/rome/sights/piazza_popolo.html
The square is a public space open at all times.